Henry E.J. Stanley

The East and the West

Our dealings with our neighbors

Henry E.J. Stanley

The East and the West
Our dealings with our neighbors

ISBN/EAN: 9783337042479

Printed in Europe, USA, Canada, Australia, Japan

Cover: Foto ©ninafisch / pixelio.de

More available books at **www.hansebooks.com**

THE
EAST AND THE WEST:
OUR DEALINGS WITH OUR NEIGHBOURS.

Essays by different Hands.

EDITED BY THE

HON. HENRY STANLEY.

February, 1865.

LONDON:

HATCHARD AND CO. 187 PICCADILLY,

Booksellers to H.R.H. the Princess of Wales.

[*The right of Translation reserved.*]

LONDON:
STRANGEWAYS AND WALDEN, PRINTERS,
28 Castle St. Leicester Sq.

INTRODUCTION.

THE perversion of ideas through the use of vague and false terms, such as policy, expediency, civilisation, military operations, &c., is the chief cause of the inability to distinguish between right and wrong which leads to the rapidly increasing number of little wars in which the country is involved. These are becoming so frequent, and are so lightly entered upon, that disasters have occurred before the country even knew that its troops were engaged. We have forced our presence upon the Japanese, and have compelled them to admit our consular jurisdiction, though its inefficacy to maintain order had been proved by experience: though Sir Rutherford Alcock has exposed its defects in the first chapter of his second volume on Japan, which is probably only a transcript of his official correspondence, no steps appear to be in contemplation for their remedy.

In 1829 M. Abel Remusat inveighed against the practice of Europeans in adopting a different standard of right and wrong out of Europe, following only their own will and pleasure; but since he wrote the following passage the evil he complained of has immeasurably increased:—" A singular race is this European race. The opinions with which it is armed, the reasonings upon which it rests, could astonish an impartial judge, if such an one could be at present found on earth. They walk the globe, showing themselves to the humiliated nations as the type of beauty in their figures, as the basis of reason in their ideas, the perfection of understanding in their imaginations. That is their only measure. They judge all things by that rule. In their own quarrels they are agreed upon certain principles by which to assassinate one another with method and regularity. But right of nations is superfluous in dealing with Orientals."

The necessity of again calling attention to these ills, is the excuse or the justification for the publication of this series of Essays. The fifth of the series does not refer to the above-mentioned subjects; but since the recent startling announcement that Convocation has already taken steps to effect intercommunion between the Church of England and the Russian Church, its publication is not less opportune.

CONTENTS.

ESSAY	PAGE
I. OUR CONSULAR SYSTEM—FOREIGN JURISDICTION IN COUNTRIES HAVING REGULAR GOVERNMENTS	1
II. MODERN CHRISTENDOM IN THE LEVANT	55
III. THE EFFECTS OF CONTEMPT FOR INTERNATIONAL LAW	111
IV. ISLAM AS A POLITICAL SYSTEM	139
V. THE GREEK AND THE RUSSIAN CHURCHES	209
VI. ON THE PROTECTION AFFORDED TO BRITISH SUBJECTS AND THEIR INTERESTS ABROAD	265

The East & the West.

I.

OUR CONSULAR SYSTEM—FOREIGN JURISDICTION IN COUNTRIES HAVING REGULAR GOVERNMENTS.

FOREIGN jurisdiction, or "extra-territoriality" as it is now sometimes called, is the right ceded by one State to another State of judging by its own officers causes arising amongst its subjects residing in the territories of the State which thus ceded part of its sovereign rights. This subject may be examined under three aspects; viz. its justice, its expediency, and its practicability.

Foreign jurisdiction is not an abstract right which can be claimed, or which is founded upon any other grounds than the good pleasure of the State which makes this concession or delegation of its rights. Neither has this system any antiquity in its favour. The *Civis Romanus*, whose memory has been invoked in support of the widest demands that could be made in behalf of British residents in foreign states, enjoyed no such privileges or immunities. His privileges were enjoyed only within the limits of the Roman Empire, and his position was like that held by the Englishman in India; though, in all probability, it did not quite amount to that, since Englishmen in India claim to be free from the jurisdiction of native magistrates, although appointed under British authority.

The custom of foreign jurisdiction arose from the grant of this privilege made by the Ottoman Sultans.

These grants, or delegations of the right of jurisdiction, were made by the Ottoman Government of its free will and pleasure, at a period of the plenitude of its power, when its greatest neighbour, the German Empire, was its tributary, and before the existence of that of Russia. This delegation of authority was in accordance with the principles of the Ottoman Government, which had already delegated civil jurisdiction amongst its Christian subjects to the Bishops at the head of the respective Churches. It is often erroneously imagined that these privileges were obtained, nay, even forced from the Ottoman Government, under treaty stipulations, on account of the name by which these privileges are known; namely, the "capitulations." This word, however, has no connexion with the verb "to capitulate;" but is derived from the Italian "*capitulazione*," having the meaning of headings or sections. At the time that the Ottoman Porte confided to the Christian embassies the power of administering the law to their subjects, this concession was not fraught with injury to the Porte. At that time the number of European subjects who came to Turkey was very small; those who came were much more under the authority of their Ambassadors and Consuls than can be the case at the present time: the capitulations contained, and still contain, provisions which have been since eluded, which prevented injury accruing to the State from the privileges which it granted. The Christian Kings, also, were more careful that these privileges should not be abused. The celebrated traveller Tavernier mentions that he had deposited a sum of money, as a security for his good behaviour, in the hands of the King's Intendant at Marseilles, before leaving France for Turkey. When the number of foreigners was very small, and was limited to men of worth and respectability, the injury caused by their immunity from subjection to the law of the land was also limited, but the introduction of steam communication and the increase of travelling has entirely altered the circumstances

The treaties, moreover, up to the present time, only sanctioned the establishment in Turkey of wholesale merchants, and did not allow of retail dealers; for it is known that a clause in a late treaty concluded between Great Britain and the Ottoman Empire, containing words sanctioning retail dealers, does not exist in the original, but was inserted in the translation by an interpreter. Such a practice would bear an ugly name if it came under the cognisance of an English court of law. The consequences have been two-fold; the foreign shopkeepers pay no taxes to the State in which they live, and are thus in a more favoured condition than the shopkeepers subjects of the country; they are also in the condition of privileged creditors and privileged debtors: secondly, the following of certain trades by foreigners, under the present system of foreign jurisdiction, renders the administration of justice impossible: all the wine-shops and coffee-houses kept by Ionians, Maltese, Greeks, and others, are closed to the police. These wine-shops are the rendezvous of robbers, murderers, and other criminals, who are more secure there than criminals were formerly in the sanctuaries of Alsatia and the Savoy. These abuses have been swept away throughout Christendom; why should Christian Governments wish to maintain them in Turkey in behalf of criminals who are not even their own subjects? for a very large proportion of the scum of Pera and Galata are only protected subjects; that is, persons abusively enjoying the immunities of the capitulations. It must be observed here, that when the Porte granted these privileges they were not intended to be applied to her own subjects; but a very large proportion of the subjects of the European Consuls, in all the countries in which the principle of foreign jurisdiction has obtained, are denationalised subjects of the State which has been deluded into making this fatal concession. The consequences to Turkey of the existence of the European community of Pera and Galata are a large accession of criminal population, a source of demoralisation, deprivation of the power of pursuing the criminals to their haunts, and absence of contribution by this community of their share of the taxes for defraying police expenses caused by themselves.

The Europeans in Turkey not being amenable to the local tribunals construe this immunity into impunity, and claim to do that which none of the inhabitants may do, and also that which is disallowed in all countries. It is but since the last treaty with Great Britain that the Porte has succeeded in excluding gunpowder from amongst those articles which may be freely traded in. Yet in all countries the trade in gunpowder must be subject to government restrictions, whether with reference to the possibility of insurrections or to the danger from fire to life and limb. Wine and spirits in a strictly Mussulman country, such as Arabia, or in countries such as Siam and Japan, are in the same category, and cannot become lawful objects of importation for the use of the inhabitants. Yet, when compensation was exacted for the sufferers by the Jiddah massacre, one of the claims brought against the Porte was put in by a Greek, not a British subject, for fifty thousand dollars for a wine-and-spirit shop. This shop probably only contained in reality a few bottles of raki and a couple of barrels of wine, of a far less value; but had it contained the quantity alleged, how can such importation be justified, whilst yearly attempts are made in Parliament by the supporters of the Permissive Bill to check the extension of the sale of spirits and the national vice of drunkenness? It must not be forgotten either, that the calamity at Jiddah was entirely brought on by the drunkenness of the *locum tenens* of the British Consul, and by his violence in enforcing his own decision of a matter which he should have referred to the Embassy at Constantinople.

The privileges conferred by what are called the capitulations, and by the successive treaties made in imitation of them with other States of Asia, were only intended to secure immunity from the summary action of local tribunals: these privileges, though placing foreigners in an exceptional position, were clearly not intended to place them in a position superior to that of the inhabitants of the country. The ancient Ottoman privileges did not, for instance, grant immunity from taxation to a large foreign community, since they not only did not contemplate, but they provided against the permanent settlement of foreigners, such as those who form the inhabitants of Pera and Galata. These people are designated by the Turks as *Vatansiz*, or people without a country, and they entirely fulfil the conditions implied by Vattel's definition of vagabonds; viz. people born of parents who have lost their domicile in one country without becoming naturalised in another. They may also be described as without a language, for they speak neither French, Italian, Greek, nor Turkish correctly, and their conversation is usually a mixture of those languages, amusing specimens of which jargon have been given by M. Théophile Gautier. But those treaties which have reference simply to the action of law-courts and police, have been wrested into the right of disregarding the laws, regulations, and social observances of the countries where those treaties exist. For instance, regulations exist in many European countries which may appear ridiculous to the inhabitants of others, but which they would not be borne out in disregarding: such as the prohibition of smoking near the sentries posted at some of the German Palaces; of keeping the head covered when the Host is passing; of whistling or playing on a musical instrument on the Sabbath in Scotland; of driving down Constitution Hill without the *entrée;* of driving fast in certain places; of walking on the grass-plots in the University quadrangles, or in various places of public resort, and the like. Now the extra-territorial treaties do not put foreigners above the law, but simply provide that infractions of the law shall be judged by or in the presence of the Consul. Yet in all the countries where these treaties hold, Europeans seem to make it a business to break through all the regulations, and disregard all the observances which they meet with.* In Turkey, for instance, they try to

---

* Francisco Suarez the Jesuit, who wrote in the middle of 1500, in his work called "Tractatus de Legibus ac Deo Legislatore," insists on the necessity of foreigners respecting the laws of the country in which they may be living, and the examples he gives include usages as well as laws of universal application. He says :—

"Moreover it is established from what has been said, that some have not rightly laid down that foreigners are bound to observe these laws only for the sake of avoiding scandal. This, indeed, is

ride fast past the Sultan's Palace, to keep their umbrellas up on passing in front of it by water: some may perhaps, some day, not dismount from their horses when the Sultan passes them in the street. In 1852, one of the English steamers which used to ply between Galata and Buyukdereh used sometimes to land passengers at Arnout-Keuy, on a quay belonging to, and in front of one of the Imperial Palaces, then occupied by Ahmed Fethy Pasha, a brother-in-law of the Sultan. Notice was given more than once to the captain of the steamer to desist from this practice, which was not only a

not true; since otherwise, if the scandal were removed, they would not be bound by these laws on their own account, or in secret places. It must therefore be said, that granted that if an actual scandal should intervene the obligation would accidentally increase, yet the scandal is not the real foundation of the obligation, but at most it is the occasion or motive which moves the legislator to enact a law, the obligation of which does not cease, even if in a particular case the motive should cease. As if arms were prohibited in such a place or time for the avoiding of broils, and if women were prohibited from adorning themselves in such mode or other, that they may not cause scandal; and nevertheless, after laws are laid down, the obligation is not so much on account of the scandal, but on their own account by reason of such laws. Therefore it stands in this case, that the necessity of avoiding scandals, and of preserving the good morals of the State, leads to the enacting of laws for all who may be found in such a place; and therefore, after the law is established, the foreigner is bound to conform to it, not only by reason of avoiding offence, but also on account of the law itself, and due subjection to it, as has been explained." (Lib. iii. cap. 33.)

breach of etiquette, but a positive nuisance, as the steamer blew all its smoke into the palace windows. The captain, however, took no heed of these warnings, and, the very day on which he had received one, came alongside the quay to land his passengers. These were met and opposed by the servants of the Palace: some of the passengers remained discreetly on board and landed higher up; but others, chiefly British subjects, landed in spite of the opposition, and some of them in the fray, in which wooden stools from the steamer were used, got their heads a little broken. One would think that they had deserved what they got, and would have been glad to let the matter end there; and so Colonel Rose, Her Majesty's Chargé d'Affaires, thought at first; but their clamour was so great that he was at length induced to make representations in favour of these disturbers of the peace, and Ahmed Fethy Pasha, in order to save the Porte further worry, paid a sum out of his own purse to satisfy the claimants, who were some Jew clerks of an English banker. It may be observed by the way, that the plying of the steamer at all was an illegality, as it came under the denomination of coasting trade.

The conduct of the Indian officers and an English woman in a mosque at Cairo a few years ago was another instance of that misbehaviour which is encouraged and brought forth by a sense of impunity. If the Pasha of Egypt had not been present, the consequences to these persons might have been fatal, and an international complication would then have ensued. A court-martial was held upon these officers, but as they were acquitted, they would not have been much discouraged from attempting the same practical jokes upon Her Majesty's Indian subjects, had not Sir Hugh Rose, the Commander-in-Chief, blamed the finding of the Court: they, however, escaped from any ill consequences of their misconduct.

In Siam, Europeans delight in standing on the small wooden bridges over the canals when any of the Ministers or great nobles are passing beneath in their barges, because this is contrary to the observances of the country; and about the year 1858 some Germans would go and shoot pigeons at one of the temples, though this amusement was forbidden. On one occasion the priests and students sallied forth against the intruders and broke their guns over their backs. They complained to Her Majesty's Consul; and though it was admitted that they were wrong in shooting the pigeons, the priests had to pay a large doctor's bill for the blows they had given.

In Japan, the murder of Mr. Richardson and the subsequent burning of Kagosima arose from the wilful disregard of warnings given, to the effect that a certain road was not to be used during a certain time. Mr. Moss got into trouble, and caused the death of a Japanese officer through his determination to shoot over ground where the Europeans had been prohibited from shooting. The French journal "La Patrie" observed at the time, that foreigners attempting to shoot in Windsor forest, or in the French forests, would at once find themselves within the grasp of the law, and that there was no reason why it should be otherwise in Japan. One of the worst cases of breach of the law is that given in a pamphlet called "Diplomacy in Japan," p. 41, in which Sir Rutherford Alcock, Her Majesty's Consul and Envoy, describes his having trespassed upon private land, not unawares, but in spite of being warned off, and the remonstrances of guardians appointed to keep off intruders. When the head of the community, placed over it to maintain the observance of law, sets such an example, what can be expected of the irresponsible, uneducated persons who form the British community in Japan? Yet the Japanese Government is made responsible for the consequences which may occur to any European who chooses to wander over the face of the country, and get himself into trouble by his unwarrantable conduct. If it be asked, "Would you have Government abandon its subjects, and let them travel at their own risk and peril?" it may be replied: Let them have in Japan the same measure of protection which Her Majesty's Government accords them in Russia, as set forth in the papers presented to Parliament in 1864, relative to the case of Mr. Anderson, who had gone to Poland and got imprisoned on suspicion which was unfounded. He was nevertheless told that he had himself to thank for having gone where he was not wanted, and that Her Majesty's Government declined to interfere in his behalf to secure him compensation for his detention.

The author of the above-mentioned pamphlet on "Diplomacy in Japan" justly observed, that the principle of extra-territoriality is most anti-humanitarian, since it implies that one nation doubts the good faith of another nation. The pretext now usually put forward in support of foreign jurisdiction in certain countries is, that their legislation, and especially their punishments, are barbarous. Taking this ground alone, the capitulations are clearly obsolete in Turkey; for capital punishment is very rare there, and the prison life is less severe than in many European countries.* The assertion that the law-

---

* "Nothing could exceed my surprise, I may say disappointment, for I had strung my nerves for a trial on going into the Bagnio, to find it by no means a horrible place, but a very quiet,

courts of any country are irregular or venal is not enough to justify the introduction of anarchy and impunity to crime which follows upon a foreign jurisdiction treaty, since this assertion may be made, and is made, in many countries of Europe and America, in which no one would think of proposing to introduce foreign jurisdiction. This accusation, moreover, is frequently brought against the consular courts. Besides which, people who leave their country for their pleasure or profit cannot expect to find all that they leave behind them; and want of confidence in a foreign law-court is a matter entirely relative and of appreciation, which might, with equal reason, lead English-

---

orderly-conducted prison. The galley-slaves of Toulon, I positively assert, are one hundred times worse off than the inmates of the Bagnio. The only point of resemblance is in their food, equally bad in each, consisting of a kind of hog-wash, sufficiently nutritious to keep the bones covered: in all other respects they differ. The galley-slaves are chained in gangs, the Bagniotes in pairs. The former must sleep on boards, the latter may sleep on beds. In Toulon dockyard no horses or steam are employed, in order that the culprits may have the harder work. In the Constantinople arsenal the number of sailors on pay, whether the fleet be in commission or not, is so great that the convicts have scarcely anything to do. The former have not the advantages of religion; within the precincts of the Bagnio are a Mosque, a Greek Church, and a Synagogue. In Toulon there are four or five thousand galley-slaves; in the Bagnio the number rarely amounts to one hundred, for a city containing about half a million of souls, and the chief rogues of the Empire."—*Admiral Slade's Travels in Turkey*, vol. i. p. 105.

men to object to being subjected to the French system, of the judge conducting the prosecution, bullying the accused, and treating him as though his guilt were already proved.

Granting that the punishments of some countries of Asia, such as China, are barbarous and cruel—as were those of Europe till a recent date—it would have been enough for the purposes of humanity if the foreign jurisdiction treaties had merely stipulated that no European should be subject to corporal punishment or torture, and that capital punishment should only be incurred for murder clearly proved, and limiting the punishments to be inflicted by local tribunals to fine, imprisonment, and banishment: the consul having the right to inspect the prisons and prison diet. It is said that imprisonment in tropical climates is too severe a punishment for Europeans: in those cases, banishment might be substituted for imprisonment: but it may be fairly urged by the Governments of Asiatic countries, that if foreigners come to their country and misconduct themselves, they must take the consequences of a climate to which nothing obliged them to expose themselves.

A few extracts from early travellers may not be out of place, as they show that the administration of justice in Asia was not barbarous, though the punishments inflicted may have been severe. At the date at which some of these were written, justice in Europe was still stumbling blindfold between red-hot ploughshares. The following extract is taken from "India in the Fifteenth Century," vol. i. p. 14:—

"It is remarkable that the administration of justice in India has been the theme of general admiration from the earliest times. Greek and Roman writers, from Diodorus Siculus downward, have eulogised it; Marco Polo witnesses on the same side; and later Arabian authors confirm their favourable testimony. El-Edrisi says, justice is a natural instinct among the inhabitants of India; and they hold nothing in equal estimation. It is stated that their numbers and prosperity are due to their integrity, their fidelity in fulfilling engagements, and to the general uprightness of their conduct. It is, moreover, on this account, that visitors to their country have increased, that the country flourishes, and that the people thrive in plenty and in peace. As a proof of their adherence to what is right, and their abhorrence of what is wrong, may be instanced the following usage: if one man owes another money, the creditor finding him anywhere, draws a line in the shape of a ring around him. This the creditor enters, and also the debtor of his own free will; and the latter cannot go beyond it until he has satisfied the claimant: but should the creditor decline to force him, or choose to forgive him, he (the creditor) steps out of the ring. Abd-er-Rezzak, also, speaking of Calicut, says,—Security and justice are so firmly established in this city, that the most wealthy merchants bring thither, from maritime countries, considerable cargoes, which they unload, and unhesitatingly send into the market and bazars, without thinking, in the meantime, of any necessity of checking the account, or of keeping watch over the goods."

Pinkerton, in his "Voyages," vol. viii. p. 377, says:—

"The mode of procedure against debtors, as described by El-Edrisi and Varthema, and which Marco Polo, before them, states to have seen carried out against the person of the King of Malabar, is confirmed by Hamilton, with slight variation."

Tavernier says, "Travels in Turkey and Persia," Paris, 1676:—

"This was not the only example which I could produce of the good order established in the whole of the East for the preservation of the goods of a foreigner, to however distant a country he may belong, who may happen to die in Turkey, or in Persia, or in India. For if these goods fall into the hands of Mussulmans, they shut them up carefully under lock and key; and they would never touch them until the true heirs of the deceased, clearly recognised as such by authentic proofs, came to claim them. If these same goods come under the direction of the English or the Dutch, they take an inventory of them, and give notice of it to the heirs, to whom they faithfully remit them; and I doubt much if, in many parts of our Europe on such occasions, so much sincerity and exactitude is made use of."

The following is from "Relations des Voyages par les Arabes dans l'Inde et la Chine, dans le Neuvième Siècle:"—

"A person who wishes to travel from one province to another obtains two papers; one from the governor, the other from the eunuch. The governor's paper serves for the road, and contains the names of the traveller and his suite, with their ages and nationality. Every one who travels in

China, whether a man of the country, an Arab, or any other, cannot dispense with a paper, by which he may be recognised. And the paper of the eunuch mentions the money and property of the traveller; and that is because there are on the roads people appointed to look into the two papers. And when a traveller passes they write for him,—Such a one, son of such a one, arrived here, of such a country, on such a day of the month, in such a year, with such property: so that a man may not lose his money or property. And if a traveller loses anything, or dies, it is known how this happened; and it is restored to him, or to his heirs after him."

Ibn Batoutah, in his " Travels," written in 1355, relates that—

" It is the custom in China to take the portrait of whoever passes through the country. This is done to so great an extent, that if a foreigner were to commit an action obliging him to fly from China, his portrait is sent to the different provinces; so that search is made, and in whatever place the man represented in the portrait is found, he is arrested."

Ibn Batoutah also mentions the custom of the Chinese of registering all the crew of sea-going junks, and of requiring an exact account of all of them from the master on his return to port. This writer also praises the precautions taken in China for the safety of merchants and travellers, a list of whom is sent on from one station to another, to ascertain the safe arrival of all of them and of their merchandise.

The *droit d'aubaine*, which is the contrary of the above-mentioned honesty with regard to the property of deceased foreigners, was protested against at a very much later date by Vattel and Grotius.

With regard to the expediency of the foreign jurisdiction, it may be said that this system is the chief cause of wars, and that it is inexpedient for any state to incur the risks of war for the sake of securing license and impunity to the criminal class —for well-behaved people do not require the intervention of the Consuls. Earl Grey has set forth in the House of Lords, what has been generally admitted, that our war with China, undertaken for the purpose of enforcing the importation of opium, weakened the Government of China, so as to produce the anarchy which now desolates that country. Lord Grey pointed out last session that the foreign jurisdiction was producing the same effects in Japan, by stimulating the license of the European community, who find themselves released from all restraint; that this trampling upon the self-respect of the Japanese must lead to war; and that, after much bloodshed and expenditure, we shall perhaps reduce Japan to a state of anarchy like that we have brought about in China. Lord Grey was derided by Ministers, but his words were confirmed before the end of the session by the publication of Sir R. Alcock's requisition for troops, which, he says, may be wanted for service in other parts of Japan. In the meantime, he has called upon the Japanese Government to provide barrack accommodation for these troops. On what footing are these troops coming? Are they friends or foes? Is this peace or war? Has the Japanese Government given permission to land these troops, or are they going without permission? If so, by all international law, this is war, and should have been preceded by a Declaration of War by Her Majesty, without which it is filibustering of the most cowardly description; and Japan is being cajoled into giving admittance to the vanguard of an army of invasion. The proceeding is so far from law and right, that it resembles the caricature of civil war. But though these troops enter Japan by means of a civil request for barrack accommodation, the consequences will most likely be tragical. In sending these troops, what object does the Government propose to itself? The eight companies which will shortly be in Japan are more than are wanted for a body-guard for the Consul, and too few for any serious military operations. They are enough to cause serious alarm to the whole Japanese nation, and apprehensions of invasion and conquest, followed by an attempt to drive out the intruders. We shall then have become involved in a war with a numerous and brave nation, in a portion of the globe the farthest removed from England—a nation which was prosperous and happy until we forced our intercourse upon them by intimidation.

It may be that these forebodings may not be realised immediately, and that England may yet have an opportunity to draw back from this false position, into which she has been brought unawares in Japan, and that the warning and example of Ashanti may be followed. In the case of Ashanti, the nation was unanimous in approving the withdrawal of the policy of Governor Pine; for the losses consequent upon pursuing it might have become very great, whilst the advantages must have been *nil*. In the case of Japan, the losses might be greater if the expedition failed, since the forces on both sides would be much greater: if successful, the expedition might gain something by plunder, but it is not easy to see what advantage the State would derive; and it cannot be supposed that the policy of England is influenced by so base a motive as the prospect of a war indemnity, however large.

No! wherever England is drawn into an aggressive war upon a weak and unoffending nation, the causes are the overbearing conduct of some agent desirous of bringing himself into notice, the greed of British settlers or adventurers, and the ignorance and indifference of the British nation, which leaves these things in the hands of the Government.

But after Lord Grey's warning last session the British nation can no longer plead ignorance of what is impending, and it will have itself to thank, and will be chargeable with the blame, if it suffers all the evils of invasion to be brought upon Japan, and a large number of our troops to be sent to that remote region, at a moment when the large quantity of troops which we have to maintain in India, Canada, and for the war in New Zealand, prevents our maintaining our ancient position in Europe, and would hamper us to a dangerous extent in case of a European war.

The following were the Resolutions proposed by Earl Grey, as recorded in the "Orders of the Day" of the House of Lords, July 1, 1864:—

" The Earl Grey—To move the following Resolutions relating to Japan :—

" 1. That the relations between this country and Japan appear to this House to be at present in a highly unsatisfactory state:

" 2. That it is shown by the papers laid before Parliament by command of Her Majesty, that the Treaty concluded between Her Majesty and the Tycoon of Japan, on the 26th of August, 1858, gives to British subjects in Japan rights and privileges which the Government of that country was avowedly reluctant to grant; and was only induced to confer upon them through dread of British naval and military power:

" 3. That the Government of Japan has also been induced

by this same fear to make with other European nations, and with the United States, Treaties generally similar to that which it has concluded with Her Majesty:

" 4. That under the above-named Treaty British subjects are entitled to claim admission into certain portions of the territory of Japan, without being subject to the jurisdiction of its Government, Her Majesty having taken upon herself the obligation of enforcing on their part good conduct and obedience to the law:

" 5. That the reports of Her Majesty's diplomatic servants show that Her Majesty has not been able to fulfil this obligation: the provisions of the statutes authorising Her Majesty's Consuls to try and punish British subjects for offences committed in Japan, and the means available for carrying these laws into effect, have proved altogether insufficient to prevent gross outrages and insults from being inflicted on the people of Japan by British subjects, and persons assuming that character:

" 6. That the animosity against foreigners, excited in the minds of the Japanese by these outrages and insults, has increased the repugnance long felt by the most powerful classes among them to increased intercourse with European nations, and has led to the perpetration of some murders, and several daring and desperate attacks upon foreigners; diplomatic servants and other subjects of Her Majesty having been among the sufferers from these acts of violence:

" 7. That the Government of the Tycoon has professed the strongest desire to prevent the commission of these crimes, and to punish their perpetrators, but has declared itself unable to do so; nor does there appear to be any reason to doubt the truth of these declarations, since two Tycoons and a Regent of Japan have themselves been murdered, and one of the principal ministers narrowly escaped the same fate, owing to the hostility they had incurred from being supposed to favour an increased intercourse with foreigners:

" 8. That in order to enforce a demand made by Her Majesty's Government of redress for the murder of a British subject, it was found necessary to undertake hostile operations against one of the Daimios; in the course of which considerable loss was experienced by Her Majesty's ships, and a large and flourishing Japanese town was burnt to the ground:

" 9. That this experience of what has already taken place, leaves little hope for the future of its being possible to avert fresh collisions between Her Majesty's subjects and the Japanese, if the existing arrangements for regulating the intercourse between them are maintained unaltered; and if such collisions should occur, they must sooner or later lead to a war which would necessarily cost many lives and much money, both to this country and to Japan; and would probably bring upon the latter the heavy calamities of general anarchy and confusion, from the destruction of its existing government; while there would be no means of creating any other authority to replace it:

" 10. That, apart from all higher considerations, the true interests of this country, and especially its permanent commercial interests, require that such calamitous results should not be risked by maintaining the existing Treaty with Japan unaltered; and that it is desirable that the provisions of this Treaty should be so modified, as to place the future intercourse of the two nations on a better footing for the future:

" 11. That it would, therefore, be advisable that Her Majesty's servants should without delay enter into friendly communication with the Government of Japan, and with the Governments of other nations having Treaties with Japan similar to our own, for the purpose of determining what changes it would be expedient to make in the provisions of these Treaties:

" 12. That an humble Address be presented to Her Majesty, to lay before Her Majesty the substance of the foregoing Resolutions, and humbly to pray that Her Majesty will be graciously pleased to take the same into her serious consideration, with the view of adopting such measures as may be found best calculated to avert war between this country and Japan, and to promote an increase of trade and friendly intercourse between the two nations, to their mutual advantage."

Lord Grey's Resolutions were called impracticable, because they were too practical, and at once cut at the root of the evil. But to see this, it required a mind used to take a wider view than one limited to the Parliamentary arena, and a Minister who cared to meet and prevent a difficulty and complications, rather than to take the chance of their not immediately arising. Instead of which, Lord Grey was answered in a party spirit. It was unfortunate that he spoke from the Opposition benches and not from the cross-benches, from which such resolutions should have proceeded. His speech and that of the Bishop of Oxford remained, however, without a reply. The Duke of Somerset avoided the question, namely, the abuses of foreign jurisdiction, and confined himself to defending the just susceptibilities of the naval officers. These are always called upon to do the dirty work of the commercial men, who, after it is done, always try to get rid of the odium attaching to it, by transferring it to the shoulders of those whom they have made tools of. Another Minister, however, denied that Lord Elgin obtained the Japanese treaty by intimidation; but Lord Elgin himself boasted, at a meeting of the Geographical Society, that he had so obtained it. It is to be regretted that an English Minister should have said,—" If we were to say to the Japanese that we would modify our Treaty, we should inspire the Japanese, as we should any Eastern nation, with an opinion of our weakness, and a belief that we were afraid of their hostility, and were endeavouring to conciliate them by needless and unworthy concessions." This is the staple argument by which newspapers, of the class designated by Mr. Trevelyan as the " rampant Anglo-Saxon press," always stave off any measure of justice which is inconvenient to them. If a concession followed after a defeat, the argument would be good, otherwise, it is one which is contrary to the truth, that human nature and the human heart are the same all over the world, and that there is no difference between the minds of Western and Eastern nations. This argument supposes what is an absurdity, that Eastern nations do not know what justice is, or what their own rights are.

Earl Russell, whilst opposing Lord Grey, in his speech virtually accepted his arguments, for he admitted the truth and force of the fourth Resolution when he said:—

"Suppose the case, and he believed such cases had occurred, where young Englishmen went beyond what they were entitled to by treaty; in those cases Sir R. Alcock would certainly have punished, if he had had the power."

Lord Russell also conceded the main facts upon which Lord Grey and his supporters founded their arguments, in making the following statement to the House:—

"That very morning he had received a long letter from Sir F. Bruce, lamenting the insolence and disregard of Chinese customs and feelings, which were exhibited by Englishmen in that country. He lamented their want of courtesy and improper behaviour to the Chinese, whom they regarded as an inferior race. He (Earl Russell) was afraid the same was the case in Japan. But conduct of that kind was not exhibited to the Chinese and Japanese alone; for he found, in a book recently published, that the same kind of conduct was practised towards the Indian race. He could not but lament that more courteous conduct was not shown by our countrymen, and that they did not pay more regard to the habits and customs of people, whom they were pleased to regard as a race inferior to their own.* All that we could do was, that

---

* "The Competition Wallah." See report of the debate in the "Morning Post," July 2, 1864. "The Times" report of this passage was inaccurate.

which had been done by men like Sir F. Bruce and Sir R. Alcock: that was, to refuse to take up the case of any of those men who had brought the evil on themselves by their own misconduct, and the use of language which was insulting to the natives, and to let them understand that it was not because they were citizens of a powerful nation that they were to be countenanced in such conduct."

This last paragraph admits all that is urged by the opponents of foreign jurisdiction; for it is not enough that men who misconduct themselves towards the natives of China and Japan should not be countenanced: it is necessary that such misconduct should be checked and punished, otherwise, as has been said above, if the obligations incurred under the foreign jurisdiction treaties be not fulfilled, this system sanctions and secures impunity, and produces anarchy; for it leaves the outraged inhabitants, whose own tribunals cannot protect them, no remedy but to take the law into their own hands: it is useless for them to appeal to the Consul, as will easily be understood, when two of Her Majesty's diplomatic officers are singled out for eulogy because they refuse their countenance and support to those who have committed an outrage. It is not every Consul who can rise to even this height of official virtue in despite of the clamour raised against him by his "subjects," who expect to be supported, right or wrong.

As in former times our merchants traded with Japan and other countries of Asia without extraterritorial treaties, it cannot be said that trade cannot be carried out without them: and assuming the statement to be true, that the Japanese desire to trade with Europe, it may safely be conjectured that the trade would have very much increased had it not been for the ill-feeling caused by the outrages which have been fostered by the foreign jurisdiction: and as this foreign jurisdiction, and the outrages and license which it is confessedly unable to repress, are likely to involve war, it cannot be denied that such jurisdiction is not expedient for the state which undertakes it.

Neither is it expedient for the individuals for whose benefit such treaties are made: it has a demoralising effect, and, setting aside outrages such as have been too frequent in Japan, it encourages dishonesty, reckless trading, and speculations far removed from the spirit of legitimate commerce. For the purposes of legitimate trade, the foreign jurisdiction treaties are far more powerful instruments than the case requires. It cannot be said that French and British subjects do not obtain their full rights, and frequently more than that, from the South American and other States, by means of the ordinary treaties and the diplomatic agents of their countries.

In order to realise what the effect of these treaties is in Asia, let the reader imagine what would be the result if the troops stationed in London ceased to be amenable to the police magistrates or to be liable to arrest by the police, and if they were amenable only to their own Colonels? Granting the best intentions to the Colonels, would the inhabitants of the metropolis feel safe, and would they long enjoy security and peace? Yet this parallel is very far from being a complete one; for the soldiers are subjected to severe discipline, and a court martial has powers far exceeding those of any consular court; and the soldiers are not like the Europeans in Asia—aliens in language, religion, and race, to the inhabitants of the country.*

The following story, told to the writer of these pages by an Ionian gentleman, is an instance of the overbearing habits and hasty recurrence to diplomatic support, engendered by the system of extra-territo-

---

* " CHINA.— Accounts have been received from Hong Kong to July 29, 1864, and other ports to corresponding dates. The following is a summary of the news : — At Hangkow a painful affair occurred on the 27th June. It appears that the Chinese there had assembled in some numbers to celebrate the Dragon feast. They crowded the river in their boats, and all the standing-ground on the riverside was occupied by spectators. A Dr. Rice, finding the lower portion of his house, which has a river frontage, crowded with Chinamen, became irritated, and fired off his revolver among them (three shots), and killed an old man who had come to town

riality. This gentleman came to Europe, and at Paris went about the streets at night singing loudly. He was interrupted by a *garde municipale*, who told him to be silent. "Is not this a free country?" he replied, and continued his singing; upon which the "municipal" arrested him in the name of the law, and locked him up for the night in the watch-house. Next day he went to Lord Normanby, to whom he had a letter of introduction, and made a complaint. The Ambassador naturally told him he had better say no more about it, and stop to breakfast with him.

After that, at Naples, he went to see the liquefaction of the blood of St. Januarius, and got to the front row, and, being of the Greek Church, he ridiculed the miracle, and expressed his feelings in an unequivocal manner by his face. The crowd of fishermen became enraged, murmured and hustled him, and would have proceeded to greater lengths if the priest had not got him out of trouble by presenting the reliquary to him, saying, "*Baciatelo, baciatelo*

to witness the spectacle. For this Rice was tried before the Consul, and he pleaded ignorance of the fact that the revolver was loaded with ball. That it was so loaded there is no doubt, as the Chinaman was shot through the heart. The Consul, however, seems to have been satisfied with the plea, as he let Rice off with a fine of 500 dollars and deportation from China. The case is considered a very painful one, as a conviction for murder would certainly have been expected had a Chinaman been the culprit and Dr. Rice the victim."—*Galignani, Sept.* 17, 1864.

con molto rispetto;" which he did, and so escaped. In this case, also, he did not scruple to make a complaint to Sir William Temple, who also naturally took no notice of it.

With regard to the third point, viz. the possibility of the state, in whose favour foreign jurisdiction treaties are made, fulfilling the obligations which it has contracted, of enforcing the observance of law and order by its subjects, it is easy to prove that, on several grounds, it is illusory to hope for any satisfactory administration of justice from the Consuls in causes arising between their subjects and the inhabitants of the country. Some of these causes of defective justice operate equally against a right decision between two parties, both of whom are subjects of the Consul: but these sort of cases are of lesser importance, since they do not lead to international complications. These causes are:—

1stly. Ignorance or deficient knowledge of the language of the country. Very few European Consuls have a knowledge of the language of the country sufficient for the purposes of justice. On the other hand it may be observed, that all the members of the Turkish commercial tribunal know French well, and that in Japan many of the officials know Dutch, and the Japanese Government has promised to provide a sufficient number knowing English. As the difficulty of different languages presses equally on all, it is more equitable that the advantage should rest with the majority, or the inhabitants of the country, rather than with the few, or the foreigners.

2ndly. A Consul under the foreign jurisdiction system is, at the same time, both judge and advocate of one of the parties. This is entirely contrary to the first principles of administration of justice. A Consul, under the ordinary treaties, is the official advocate of the subjects of the power which he represents, and it is difficult for him to divest himself of this quality when acting under the extra-territorial treaties. Under the Turkish treaty, where the defendant is a European subject in a criminal trial, the cause should be tried before the Turkish judge, and the Consul can only act as assessor, and see that the trial is fair, and give his opinion with regard to the sentence: but in many cases this has been over-ridden, and the Consul constituted sole judge.

3rdly. The persons who hold the office of consul, which, under these treaties, is that of judge, are generally unfitted for, and unworthy of, these posts. The smallness of the sum voted by Parliament does not allow Her Majesty's Government to secure the services of first-rate men for these posts; but, on the other hand, the Government may be blamed for the multiplication of consulships, and for frequently appointing men who, it must know, ought not to be trusted with such large powers. Many Consuls are appointed simply because they happen to be in the country, to which they have come as adventurers, and their services are cheaper than those of a man sent out from England.* Trading is incompatible with the functions of a Consul exercising foreign jurisdiction. Levantines, or subjects of the country, are not only totally unfit for the post of consul, but their appointment is a violation of treaty; nevertheless, many such are to be found in the Foreign Office list. If Consuls are wanted in so many places, and the means are wanting for appointing proper and respectable persons, these appointments should be filled up by persons with the title of consular agents, without any judicial power, and whose functions should be limited to correspondence with higher officials of their Government.

4thly. The Consuls are, in general, on terms of too great social intimacy with the subjects over

* For instance: an individual escaped from a certain country leaving behind him creditors, some of whom he had ruined; the debts filed against him amounted to 7715*l*. 14*s*. He arrived in another country, where he managed to get appointed Her Majesty's Consul, and, aided by his official position, he enriched himself. His creditors, however, have been unable to obtain any money from him. This person has retired from the post, after filling it longer than was good for the country.

whom they are set, for them to be able to act impartially towards them in the administration of justice.*

5thly. The Consuls are, in general, not men of sufficient position to command the respect of the merchants; and the forms of English law are such as to leave the Consuls little power to check outrages and misconduct on the part of their subjects.

6thly. The position of a Consul, even the best of the British Consuls, cannot be compared to that of an English magistrate, who has an English press, audience, and clerk, to guide and check him. If the newspaper press so often complain of Justices' justice, what an outcry would they not raise if they had an insight into Consuls' justice!

7thly. Where foreign jurisdiction exists there are from ten to twenty Consuls with equal powers, so that when subjects of various European states are engaged in a case, the confusion is endless and justice hopeless, each Consul standing out firmly for his own "subject."

8thly. Even if a Consul were disposed to administer strict justice it would be most difficult for him to do so, on account of the clamour which would be raised by a community such as the European

* A similar objection has been made to the multiplication of County-court Judges in England.

community in Japan. The case of Mr. Moss is an example of this, and others could be mentioned.

9thly. The Consuls being frequently removed from one post to another, cannot be equally cognisant with a local tribunal of the antecedents of the persons they have to deal with.

10thly. The Consuls have no police at their disposal sufficient for carrying out the law and maintaining order.

The above-mentioned circumstances are causes enough to render the action of the consular body ineffective for the purpose of maintaining order amongst their subjects, many of whom, it must be remembered, are the outcasts of Europe, especially at Constantinople and Alexandria. Unless, therefore, a very great reform is made—and the circumstances do not allow of much reform—the Governments exercising foreign jurisdiction cannot flatter themselves that they fulfil their obligations in this respect. It may be doubted whether the very questionable justice administered by the Consuls is of any advantage to Europeans in civil cases; and the only persons who profit by the system are the ruffians, assassins, and thieves, that render the streets of Pera and Galata unsafe after dark.

England, Austria, Italy, and Greece, have the honour, at Constantinople and in Egypt, of protecting the worst malefactors: the robberies and murders committed at Pera are generally attributable to Maltese, Ionians, Croats, Italians, and Greeks. The French Consuls in Turkey are, on the whole, those who give least cause of complaint in this respect. People in England will hardly believe or understand the impunity and freedom of malefactors in Pera. The following anecdote will best illustrate it:—The dragomans of the consulates go every day to the chief police-office, and claim their respective subjects who may have been taken up during the night on their predatory excursions. On one occasion, the British or the Austrian dragoman—it does not matter which—claimed a thief, who, in the usual course, was released. Two days later, a merchant had a large sum of money in his house, and having been warned that his house was likely to be attacked, he applied for and received four Turkish policemen to guard his premises. An attempt to break in was made in the night by a band of burglars, who did not know the house was guarded: resistance was made, pistols used, and two of the burglars killed. The dead bodies and the captured survivors were brought to the police-station; and next morning, when the dragomans came to claim their own, the Zabtieh Pasha conducted one of them to the dead burglar, and said, "There is your subject: you had better have left him in my hands two days ago, and he would not have had an opportunity of returning to his evil ways, and be in the state in which you now see him."

The establishment of British Consular Judges at Constantinople and Smyrna has not much improved matters: more of the tedious and expensive forms of English law may have been introduced; the rest remains much as before. Now, however, that we are no longer burdened with those most litigious of mortals, the Ionians, there will be much less for those courts to do; and perhaps they, as well as several of the small consulships, may be abolished.

Some idea of the discretion of the British Consular Court at Constantinople may be formed from the following facts:—At the end of 1859 a Greek vessel left Constantinople for the Black Sea, and either on account of contrary winds, or for some other reason, it anchored off a small village in the Bosphorus, near the entrance of the Black Sea; and the master and crew all went on shore to while away the time at a *café*. During this time an English tug-steamer came by, and seeing no one on board the Greek vessel, although it was in port—for the whole of the Bosphorus is a port—considered it as abandoned, and towed it back to Constantinople.

The Greek crew were much surprised on finding their vessel had disappeared, and returned to Pera, where they discovered what had become of their vessel, which was detained by the Tug Company under a claim for salvage. They then applied to their Consul, who wrote to Admiral Slade, the Turkish commander of the port, asking him to cause the restitution of the vessel. This Admiral Slade did; but the Tug-steamer Company, choosing to act for themselves, collected a body of Ionians, and sent them to board the vessel and eject the crew. The Greek Consul again referred to Admiral Slade, who was obliged to have the Greek vessel retaken from the Ionians for its owners by a Turkish man-of-war's boat. Now, it will appear hardly credible, but it is true, that an action was brought by the Tug-steam Company against Admiral Slade for his proceedings in this matter. And this action against a Turkish official (for Admiral Slade's British nationality had nothing to do with his official acts) was entertained by the Consular Court; and, though Admiral Slade denied the competency of the Court, it gave a judgment against him for damages.

Some idea may be formed as to the possibility of enforcing the observance of law and order in various Asiatic countries by means at the disposal of the European Consuls, by an inquiry into the administration of justice in our own possessions in Asia: it may be expected that the law will be better administered to our fellow-subjects of Asiatic origin by English courts of law and magistrates, than it would be in the case of Asiatic foreigners by European Consuls. This comparison may be drawn by a few extracts and references to cases which have lately occurred.

The Reverend G. P. Badger, late Government Chaplain in the Presidency of Bombay, writes:—

"Varthema's reiterated encomium on the impartial administration of justice, wherein he corroborates the testimony of ancient Greek and Roman authors, reveals another striking feature in the Indian polity at this period. That no declension in that respect has resulted from the supersession of the old native tribunals by British legislation cannot be doubted; nevertheless, the two systems are frequently contrasted by the people, to the decided disparagement of the latter. The chief defect complained of, however, is the comparative tardiness of our law; for, under the Oriental mode of procedure, punishment follows hard on the offence, and cases are disposed of without the intervention of those intricate forms and delays, and without the heavy fees, which seem inseparable from a British law-court. There are, unquestionably, many among the better-informed natives who appreciate the even and solid justice ultimately aimed at and dispensed; but the masses revert with regret to the good old days, when awards were attainable in much less time, and at far less cost, than at present. This subject reminds me of a wealthy Arab pearl-merchant from the Persian Gulf, whom I met at Muskat upwards of two years ago, and who occasionally formed one of a party of evening visitors, whose opinions I frequently endeavoured to elicit on points connected with British policy in the East. The theme under discussion was the administration of justice in India; in the course of which the Arab merchant, who was well acquainted with Bombay, spoke as follows, as nearly as I can remember his words:—There can be no doubt that the Government of the English is the best in the world, and no Eastern Government can be compared to it. Their law, too, is excellent; and their judges and magistrates incorruptible: still, there are serious drawbacks in the way of obtaining justice. Knowing this by experience, I long forbore pressing a case against a man who was indebted to me to a large amount; but a Parsee acquaintance eventually persuaded me to put myself into the hands of an English lawyer, who, he was sure, would get my claim settled promptly and economically; and, moreover, gave me a note of introduction to his legal adviser. Thanking him for his courtesy, but still wary of the machinery of the law, I took the note to a Banyan, and begged him to read it for me. It contained this sentence: 'My dear ——, I send you a good fat cow; milk him well.' I need not tell you that my suspicions were confirmed, and that I preferred a voluntary compromise with my debtor to an involuntary milking at the hands of the English advocate. The anecdote, whether true or fabricated, is illustrative of a very common notion among the natives respecting the obstacles in the way of securing prompt justice from a British court of law in India."*

Reference to the pages of the "Competition Wallah," and especially to the mention there made of the trial of the missionary, Mr. Long, for his translation of the Bengali play "Nil Darpun," would

---

* Introduction to Varthema's Travels, p. lxxiv.

go far to prove that English law-courts in Asia are by no means the same as English law-courts in England.* The extraordinary charge delivered by Sir Mordaunt Wells at Mr. Long's trial could not have been delivered in England. The author of the "Competition Wallah" has quoted the strongest passages in "Nil Darpun," and the reader will be able to form his own opinion of them, which will assuredly not lead him to agree with the epithet of obscene, which was affixed to that publication; neither will he find anything in it to justify the sentence of one month's imprisonment inflicted on

---

* It would appear from the following, that legislation as well as the administration of the law in India is falling off.

Act I. of 1849 enacts, sect. 2, that "all British subjects, all employés, and *all* persons who *shall have dwelt* six months in British India, whether apprehended there or *elsewhere*, shall, when delivered to a magistrate, be amenable to the law for *all* offences committed by them *within any foreign* territory; and may be committed to trial on the like evidence as would warrant their commitment in India."

It follows that a Dutchman, who thirty years ago passed six months in Bombay, might be tried by the Court of Singapore for an affray or a nuisance committed by him in Bangkok. What would the Dutch say to this; or *we*, if the parts were inverted?

So if he had never been in British India before he committed the offence, but had fled after its commission to Singapore, he would be safe for five months and twenty-nine days, but would be liable to be tried under the Act as soon as he had completed his six months' residence.

So though the offence had been committed not in the country which gave him up, but some other. Thus the Dutchman, who

Mr. Long: especially when he is told that the "Report of the Indigo Commission" contains far more severe strictures upon the indigo planters than any contained in "Nil Darpun."

It is not surprising that outrages should occur in Japan, when a case like the following could occur in the British port of Singapore, in the year 1861 or 62. The master of a British merchant-vessel, at anchor in that port, saw two Malays approaching his vessel in a boat, in the daytime. It is not clear what he could have apprehended from only two men. However, he hailed them, and then took a gun and

once passed six months in Singapore, might be tried in Calcutta for an offence committed in Siam, if given up by the King of Burmah.

The offences are those for which he might be committed for trial in India. Therefore an Arab might be seized and tried in Bombay for *buying a slave* in Egypt. Further, a Siamese subject, who had passed six months in Singapore, might be sent to the Court of Singapore for trial for a crime committed in his own country.

In the former cases, foreign states would have a right to object to our thus dealing with their subjects for offences not committed *in our territory*. In the latter, the tax-payer might object to the expense of punishing such offenders. The Act does not require that all such cases shall be tried, but gives the Government the power to have them tried. It leaves to the good sense of the Executive the task of neutralising the extravagance of the Legislature. What a wide door for abuse! The act is too wide, both as respects offences and offenders: the former should be limited to acts held to be crimes by all nations, the latter to subjects of the British Crown.

fired, first at one and then at the other, knocking them both over. One remained in the boat wounded, the other fell over into the sea and was seen no more. As the body of this man was not to be found, the master of the merchant-vessel was only put upon his trial for shooting with intent to injure. Notwithstanding that the indictment was so much less serious than the circumstances of the case admitted or required, the jury recommended the prisoner to mercy, and the judge passed so slight a sentence upon him that the governor had to urge him to reconsider it, and to inflict a severer punishment.

At Pulo-Pinang an Arab had left a large sum of money for the Malay schools, under the care of trustees. These trustees, having disagreed amongst themselves, the matter was brought before the court, in the time of the predecessor of the present Recorder. The result was, that the capital was and is detained by the Court, and the interest has been applied to Christian schools. Now, English law is clear upon the duty of respecting the intentions of testators, as has been proved especially in the case of the trusts founded under Lady Hewley's will.*

The mate of a European merchant-ship had murdered his captain, and was condemned to be hanged.

* See the case of the Attorney-General against Shore.

There was nothing in the case to excuse the murderer, or to raise any sympathy in his favour; yet some Europeans regretted his execution, and said it was so horrible that a white man should be hanged, on account of the bad effect it would have upon the natives. The same feelings made the Singapore merchants object to the employment of European convicts in their town. Now, as the natives know very well that there are criminals amongst the Europeans as well as amongst the people of other nations, the only effect of giving way to these prejudices would be to lead the inhabitants of Asia to suppose that our justice was one-sided, if they never saw a sentence carried out upon a European.

It is, however, chiefly in minor matters that European administration presses hard upon the people of Asia; for whilst, throughout that region, the officers of Government are always accessible — and in many countries petitions can be presented to the Sovereign himself — British officials are almost inaccessible, or their manner of receiving petitioners is such as to deter people from presenting themselves. What the people of Asia expect, and what they get from their own governors, may be illustrated by the following examples:—Viscount Escayrac de Lauture relates, in his travels in the Soudan, that he was sitting with a Turkish official, and that an Arab came with a complaint, and preluded it with a long account of his genealogy. Monsieur de Lauture asked the Turk afterwards why he had not cut him short, and the answer was, "If I had not listened to the whole of his story he would have gone away and said that I would not do him justice." Mr. Eastwick, the late Secretary of Legation in Persia, relates in his book that a Persian said to him, "You would do to govern in Persia, for you know how to listen to a man's story." It may be said that the time of officials ought not to be wasted, but there might be a medium between the two practices. In England we recognise the principle of a fair hearing, when an Old Bailey lawyer takes up the time of the Court with apparently irrelevant questions to the witnesses; and the judge reminds the prisoner that he has had a fair trial and a patient hearing.*

But the climax of lawlessness may be said to have been attained in the following occurrence, which, as it took place in Her Majesty's dominions, gives the measure of what may be expected in China and Japan. Some sailors of some Queen's ships went on shore on leave, and came across a Hindoo proces-

* It is a pleasure to be able to mention, amongst others who uphold the dignity of English law and justice, and cause them to be appreciated in Asia, such men as Sir Benson Maxwell the Recorder of Pinang, and Mr. Thompson, late Queen's Advocate in Ceylon.

sion, and tried to force their way with it into a temple. They were repulsed with some bruises. Next day the crews resolved to avenge this affront, and a party of officers and men set out in the evening, and, with a regularity which would have done them credit in the presence of the enemy, left men with the boats and outposts on the road, and proceeded to the temple to force their way in. A fight ensued with sticks and stones; some of the Hindoos were hurt, a lieutenant had two front teeth knocked out, and a seaman had his arm broken. The magistrate of the place wrote to the captain to complain of the riotous conduct of his men; and the captain wrote an intemperate letter in reply, regretting that more of the natives were not hurt instead of his own men.*

If this could go unpunished within the Queen's dominions, how much more likely is it that outrages will be committed in countries where the foreign jurisdiction treaties secure impunity to offenders? If this outrage had been committed in a foreign country, compensation would probably have been claimed for the injured officers and seamen.

These treaties could hardly work effectively, even

* The time and place of this occurrence are not given here, since the writer is not attacking individuals, but the anomalies of the foreign jurisdiction, and the abuses which are its necessary results.

with the best machinery; and they are always open to the objection that they degrade and lower the governments of the countries in which they exist, and create an unduly privileged position for the Consuls and subjects of the powers in whose favour they are made. What is, moreover, the machinery actually at work for carrying out the obligations of these treaties?—Consuls having the power of magistrates, but without legal training or social *status*, with no police to speak of to carry out their orders, or to cause them to be respected. The Consuls themselves are generally either traders or adventurers, or persons who have failed in other professions. In the Levant many Consuls are pluralists; that is, they represent, in their own persons, several powers. On official reception-days such a Consul pays several visits successively to the Governor, merely going out of the room to change his decorations, and having himself again announced as Consul of another country: such an official is named in Levantine French, " *Un Consul de plusieurs potences.*" Readers of the "Times" will not have forgotten the scandal caused by the sham insurance of the " Poseidon ;" a ship imagined for the purpose by one of Her Majesty's Consuls. The offender in this case was unfortunate in being discovered, and that, too, by an insurance company, which would not allow the case to be hushed up;

otherwise, he was not a singular instance of what is to be met with in the consular body. It was from this individual, and others of the same calibre, that Lord Carlisle and Mr. Senior drew the facts with which they enlightened the world, after a tour too hurried for anything to be gained by their own observation, but during which they made themselves into reservoirs, to be filled by every one they came across, without selection.

Meantime, until the obsolete capitulations are done away with in Turkey, and the treaties with other countries altered, so as not to be, as at present, sources of war and of impunity for crime, without any counterbalancing benefit, the Foreign Office should aim at diminishing the number of consulships, so as to be able, with the means allowed by Parliament, to improve the more important consulships, and to fill them with responsible and respectable persons. Official persons have derided Lord Grey's Resolutions as being impracticable. But this is saying, in other words, that the subject was new to them; that they had not yet reflected on the damage done by the extra-territorial system; that they had not yet considered how it was to be remedied; that public attention had not yet been drawn to the subject; and that pressure had not yet been brought to bear upon them, so as to make them feel the necessity of doing something: and on the rule of "*Quieta non movere*," it is impracticable to alter anything until the necessity for doing so has been clearly demonstrated and loudly called for. Thus it is at present impracticable for Government to enforce upon Railway Companies the establishment of communication between guards and passengers. This benefit will eventually be obtained, but not until other calamities have roused the public to make a greater outcry.*

Another suggestion deserves the attention of the Foreign Office, as it may avert much mischief; and in order to carry it out, it requires nothing more than the assent of the Foreign Office to the proposition. Whereas it is not competent to one magistrate to appoint another person as magistrate, but a person can only obtain such a nomination through the Lord-lieutenant; it is not fitting that when a Consul, under the foreign jurisdiction system, goes away from his post on leave, he should be able to leave in his place, as acting consul, any person whom he may select and recommend to the Foreign Office as fit for the duty: since the persons chosen by Consuls to act in their absence are necessarily, in general, unknown to the Foreign Office: they are frequently

* The need of these calamities may perhaps be superseded by the act of the Queen.

persons without education, and of low position; and they are necessarily without that feeling of responsibility which attaches to a person in a regular service, who has something to lose by misconduct. It should, therefore, be established for the future that the *locum tenens* of the Consul should be limited in his functions to correspondence with his superiors; and that more important matters should remain in abeyance until the return of the Consul: or if there were much business, that the Embassy should depute a competent person to act in the absence of the Consul, but that the appointment of an acting consul should not depend so much, as heretofore, upon the Consul. The French system provides against this defect, by the appointment of a *Chancelier* to each consulate. But this would add greatly to the expense of consulships, many of which already have not work enough for one man. This suggestion might seem capable of recommending itself as it stands; but it derives additional weight from the fact that it was the selection by Mr. Coles, Her Majesty's Consul at Jiddah, of Mr. Page, to be acting consul in his absence, which led to the massacre at Jiddah. Mr. Page was of a very humble station in life, and was known as one who drank before this occurrence. The massacre was represented as a fanatical outbreak, but it originated solely in national feelings, and the irritation caused by the precipitate—and, as the people of the country had good reason to think—unjust hauling down of the Ottoman flag from a vessel on which its owner, an Ottoman subject, had hoisted it; and by the subsequent drunken abuse and insults heaped upon the people by the acting consul.

This calamity would not have occurred if this unfit person had not been put in a position which enabled him to provoke it; and it cannot be said that British interests would have suffered by the post having remained vacant during the Consul's absence; nor even if the post were abolished altogether: for there are no English at Jiddah, nor British trade, though British goods find their way there very well from Egypt, unassisted by the intervention of Englishmen.

It is a mistake to suppose that the appointment of Consuls can produce trade: where no prohibitive duties interpose, goods follow the laws of supply and demand, and the demand depends upon their quality more than upon consular protection. A very large quantity of British goods find their way to Central Asia by means of Greek houses in Persia: that trade is unprotected, and stands on its own basis; some years ago it received a check from the covetousness of some dishonest parties, who sent out inferior goods, the colours of which would not stand:

this act discredited British goods very considerably in the markets of Central Asia.

If persons unfitted by education and position are appointed as consuls and acting consuls, they not only do disservice to their own State, but the appointment is most offensive to the country in which it is made; and it is not fair upon the high officials of the countries we have been speaking of, who are remarkable for their courtesy and urbanity, to force them to receive men entirely deficient in manners and education—such as might perhaps pass muster at a small trading-port in Europe, where their duties are confined to attending to shipmasters and bills of health, but who are unfit to be brought into that frequent contact with the governor of a province which the foreign jurisdiction treaties render necessary. This is not merely an Asiatic prejudice, for a paragraph has been lately going the round of the papers to the effect that the last Japanese Embassy to Europe (in 1864) was composed of persons of low extraction. If it is so, the Japanese Government has been acting on the principle of reciprocity.

Amongst other vexations to the Japanese, is that caused by the exigencies put forward by the European Consuls for lodging in the temples.* Similar

* "Diplomacy in Japan," pp. 10–15.

requisitions are often made in other countries; and this contrasts ill with the niggardly reception given to embassies and deputations from Asia to England, whose extensive relations with Asiatic countries occasionally force the inhabitants of those countries to have recourse to England.

An article appeared in the Brussels "Revue Trimestrielle," of July 1863, from the pen of Monsieur John Ninet, a Belgian Vice-consul in Egypt, which deserves the attention of those who wish to study the action of the Consuls in the Levant. The extracts which follow will show that the baneful effects of the foreign jurisdiction have not been overstated in the foregoing pages.

II.

MODERN CHRISTENDOM IN THE LEVANT.

The following Extracts are translated from an Article written by M. JOHN NINET, *a Belgian Vice-Consul, and Acting Consul at Alexandria, and published in the Brussels " Revue Trimestrielle," July* 1863.

No doubt that, from a Christian point of view, and taken in the abstract, certain usages of Eastern peoples present themselves to European criticism as real defects and as great vices; but with a little more of evangelical charity, perhaps, we should judge them less severely. We should take more into account the influences of origin and climate, and the material necessities and social obligations derived from these usages; we should take into consideration men and circumstances; we should be able to distinguish what is good; and in finding an explanation of what shocks our observation, we should be less harsh in attacking, and more sincere in our judgments. We should at length arrive at this conclusion, however unedifying it may be, that, under the cloak of civilisation with which we deck ourselves, we, modern Christians, hide a mediocre body, and a mind more full of hypocrisy than we are disposed to admit.

If, after a general awakening, the Mussulman, Buddhist, and idolatrous nations were suddenly and spontaneously to discover that they could not live without railways, without fermented liquors, without fashionable goods from Paris and London, without European fabrics, &c., and if they opened both their ports and their treasures to the precipitate incursion of the products of manufacturing Christendom, Christendom at the outset would ask for nothing more. The question of religion would very readily, and with joy, be left on one side, saving that it would be brought in later for the purpose of satisfying fresh appetites, sprung from the prey already devoured.*

But we have not arrived at this point. From the outset, and on many points of the globe, the fault was committed of not taking the bull by the

---

* The author is proved to be right in asserting that Christianity is made the pretext and the cloak for avarice and greed, by the fact that the adoption of it has not saved the New Zealanders from the greed and spoliation of the colonists.—*Translator.*

horns. The bale of cloth was sometimes put on the robe of the Missionary, and the Cross was clumsily sent as the forerunner of the yard measure, with its sequel of odious consequences. The religious feelings of those nations designated as barbarous were wounded, and remained timid and suspicious. From that point to violence and reprisals the distance was not great. Politics became mixed up in the matter, and cannon made itself heard. Christendom, which especially distinguishes itself in the art of imposing its laws, and of mutual destruction by fire and sword, declared the nations who were rebellious against its civilisation to be enemies of the Cross. Thus the human race has dug the abyss which separates nations, from whom true progress might have obtained everything, if no attempt had been made upon their beliefs; to which they are, and have the right to be, as much attached as we are to ours.

The Japanese, for instance, obstinately refuse to open their country to us. Our inferiors in many accessory branches of manufacturing art, they are our equals and superiors in many others, especially having regard to their wants and tastes. The products of Europe tempt them but little; and if by reason of some treaties imposed upon them, rather than negotiated, they receive a few specimens adapted to their consumption, it will be in order to imitate them at first, and at the end of a short time to surpass them in quality and cheapness.

Ancient sumptuary laws have early rendered the inhabitants of those islands of a remarkable simplicity in their manners, which makes them reject as useless those gold and silver trinkets to which Christians attach so much value. Moreover, spirituous liquors in Japan are met by a prohibitive duty (35 per cent ad valorem), as being the source of corruption of the people, and of evils of which this nation is still ignorant. In short, they consider themselves happy as they are, governed by their own laws, whether good or bad; they can live, and do live without us, and beseech us earnestly to leave them alone.

It is not that they disdain all the advances of the Christians indiscriminately. In times long gone by, missionaries from old Europe penetrated into the country, where, thanks to a protecting tolerance, they made numerous proselytes. The Dutch, those cold calculators, merchants in their very souls, whose admirals, ministers, and residents, forestalled the reign of the dollar, whilst acting as buffoons at the court of the Tycoons, had the exclusive monopoly of Japanese commerce for a long time within their hands. But instead of upholding the standard of the Cross above love of lucre, these austere Protestants, preferring Mammon to the religion of mercy, joined with the inhabitants, and assisted them to massacre thirty thousand Christians belonging to the country! If at that time civilisation showed itself but little scrupulous in the choice of means, when its material interests were at stake, has one the right to require or expect much from it at the present time? It is, therefore, very allowable to lift with a sceptical hand the curtain which conceals its real designs. There is a desire for the silk, the tea, the wax, and the camphor of the Japanese; and it is sought to convert them to the products of Europe—to its stuffs, its fashions, its spirits . . . . let us say it—to its vices. The nation will enrich itself, it is said, and become civilised. Let us be more honest, and add—it will first become corrupt, will become weak, and will be divided, and, sooner or later, it will be conquered.

* * * * *

Meantime, all the European powers are at present seized with a mania for negotiating with Japan. His Excellency Mr. Stampfli, himself, the President of the Swiss Republic, has not escaped from the reigning epidemic. He has just sent to the Tycoon a watchmaking mission, at a great cost, charged with offering to this Prince, who is said to be dead, the compliments of Switzerland—*Absinthe* of Couvet, cigars which do not draw, watches of Geneva, and bears from Berne: the whole under the Dutch flag, and in exchange for a treaty of commerce to be negotiated.*

Here is certainly wherewithal to hasten the success of the great humanitarian cause; and if the Japanese do not submit to these wonderful efforts of modern civilisation, it must be admitted that their ears are very dull and very long.

The case has been pretty nearly the same with Turkey and the Osmanlys; every one uttered maledictions and invectives against them. Even now, it is the fashion to make their funeral oration from time to time, accompanied by kicks, after the manner of the ass in the fable; unless, however, when the requirements of a doubtful policy draw upon them the honour of flattery as exaggerated as it is ridiculous. There is no middle term: the club or incense. But incense is what is least made use of.

Is it then forbidden, or in bad taste, to speak

---

* The spirit of gain and coveteousness on this occasion made the Swiss as regardless as others of infringing the rights of the Japanese, and as eager to put an unjust pressure upon them as though they had never learned the lessons of William Tell, or as though their own existence as a nation did not depend upon the more or less that ideas of justice may still prevail in Europe.— *Translator.*

the truth concerning the Mussulmans? and may one not do so without being taxed with partiality by some, with lukewarmness in religion by others?

When a man writes what he knows, and publishes that which is fact, he deserves, at least, some good will; and his doing so is, at any rate, worth more than perorations on all occasions, upon things which people have not seen, and of which they are ignorant, merely for the sake of putting in a word and making a noise.

In the presence of the surprising and various events which have been unrolled before our eyes since the painful Eastern question has been invented by a diplomacy in quest of strong emotions, since that hidden power has made a rampart of it, behind which she shelters the most unavowable theories of intervention and annexation, would it not be fair to inquire, in good earnest, whether the *head*, in this so-called corruption, has compromised the soundness of the body? Whether the head and body have not, on the contrary, been cured at Sebastopol? The efficacity of the remedy applied in the Crimea cannot, however, be considered doubtful. There were there many great doctors—too many, perhaps —assembled later at the Congress of Paris. Now, if the patient is better—which seems to be admitted by everybody, the collateral heirs alone excepted

—would it not be urgent to allow him a better diet, more air, more sun, and more freedom in his exercise?

* * * * *

Since the Crimean war things have changed their aspect. Those events have been a lesson, and the Ottomans have learned that they had friends, and that their religion was admitted to the same privileges which are accorded to other beliefs which respect themselves, and know how to make themselves respected. The veil which interested hands had extended during so long a time over Turkey has fallen for ever, and political life has been restored to a nation which it would be unjust not to recognise as worthy of the sympathies of Europe.

Let us now examine, without passion, political or religious, impartially and coolly, which side has been in the wrong, and, leaving the Crescent on one side, inquire how civilisation, including the rayah element, has behaved itself towards the Mussulmans.

Let us first acknowledge that the most patriarchal hospitality has ever been held in honour by the Mussulmans, for whom it is a sacred duty, which they have never forgotten to practise towards whoever has partaken of their bread and salt. There are features in the characters of nations which may pass for exaggerated, and which sometimes belong more to the realm of legend than to reality based upon facts. But the noble virtue which we are here speaking of has nothing of a usurped reputation: it is as lively with the lowly as with the great; and it is general, for it knows no distinction between enemies and friends, believers and unbelievers: it sees only brothers in those who shelter themselves under the tent of the nomad, or who take their places at the table of the powerful.

*　　*　　*　　*　　*

Here, then, is a national virtue acknowledged and proved; and which has all the more value since, in the progress which Turkey is going to make, it will be one of the bases absolutely necessary to success. A primitive and hospitable nation is near touching the goal which the march of humanity lays down for it.

Those Europeans who have traversed the Levant as patient and conscientious observers—those who have lived in it, and have directed commercial establishments during many years, will acknowledge with us the manifest inferiority in which the Mussulmans have been placed with regard to protected rayahs and other Christians. This remark applies particularly to the great centres of population, where the European community, being more compact, gives to its members more confidence, and by the same stroke diminishes their discretion and their reserve in their habitual relations with the non-Christian subjects of the Porte.* The Levantines themselves—and here we mean Catholics, Copts, &c., natives of the country, are sometimes no better treated than their Mussulman fellow-countrymen; and they feel all the more the effects of the supe-riority which the Europeans arrogate to themselves, since they ought, on the contrary, to expect protection on their part with regard to the Mussulmans. In six-tenths at least of quarrels provoked by daily contact, and which are brought before the consulates or submitted to the jurisdiction of the *bashaga* (police), the Christians are the aggressors. Eight cases out of ten are decided in their favour. To curse one's neighbour's religion, even in joke—the Jew the Christian's, the Mussulman the Jew's, the Christian the Rayah's—is a habit unhappily too deeply rooted in this country, where creeds are as varied as the kinds of animals in Noah's ark. And what a superfluity of base expressions fill the public vocabulary in these cases! It can hardly be confessed that these are the first phrases which the new-

* After the Treaty of Paris a Turkish squib represented a Syrian Christian insulting a Mussulman, who replied, "How dare you do that? I am your equal now!"—*Translator.*

comer hastens to learn to stammer. It seems as though there were a resolution to treat the inhabitants as roughly as possible in all the divers circumstances of business life. We ask, Of what advantage are the benefits of that civilisation, of that Christianity especially, of which we boast with just cause, if we are only able at the outset to discover in it a pretext to oppress the weak, and whatever person does not think like ourselves?

We are not exaggerating. Europeans all, whoever they may be, show themselves inclined to the sweets of this petty despotism, which makes them consider the usages of foreign countries to which their lot brings them as absurd and heavy to be borne. They hasten, it might be said, to break the bonds which, in their own countries, restrained them within the limits of law and justice.

Look at that fellah, in whose barley you go shooting without license — you and your dogs — whose garden you visit, filling your pockets. He is silent for the most part, to avoid the buffet which your ready hand has in store for him, or the curses which your mouth already murmurs. Would you act thus in Europe, where the game-laws are as numerous as they are vexatious, and where the rights of property are respected under pain of the severest penalties? From the rights conferred by the capitulations which bear hard upon the self-respect of this nation, we rush to the abuse; and if some inhabitant, injured in that which is dearest to man—his national and religious dignity—mildly ventures to make a very natural observation, "*Civis Romanus sum,*" is your reply, whilst you humiliate him with your look and gesture.

Whilst the charcoal-dealer, as was said at Paris in 1830, is master in his own house—whilst the London cockney considers his home as his castle, can we take it ill that the Mussulmans ask for reciprocity? Their rich empire, so full of resources, so fertile, so well situated, so productive, calls us to its bosom: is it, then, to require too much of the European emigration, as well as of the native Christians, that the one and the other should behave decently towards the nation which to-day tolerates them and might love them to-morrow? If Islamism is everywhere pitied as the representative of a world of relative ignorance and barbarity, would not our duty as Christians be to seek to ameliorate it by good conduct and by example? If, in short, Europeans, more skilled and gifted with great perspicacity, have discovered a weak side in this nation, developed by a corrupted financial system, by salaries too low for responsible posts, by a relatively poor mode of living, is it very worthy of more advanced nations to speculate upon these faults and to enrich themselves by converting them into vices? Example, such is the flag of the real pioneers of civilisation, that which would inevitably lead the Ottomans into a path more analogous to our habits and customs, and more favourable to our dealings with them. This nation, though belonging to different origins, is not the less intelligent, nor less capable of reform and progress.

Less than fifty years ago, the simple word of a Mussulman merchant was worth a bond in the bazar; his *yes*, with a clasp of the hand, was his signature, his acceptance; and on payment becoming due, the collector of the Christian merchant never left the counter of his debtor without being satisfied.

Now it is no longer so, or, rather, such is no longer the rule, but the exception. Consular protections abusively granted, and the resources of our vitiated civilisation, have altered the usages of the good old time. The buyers in the bazar accept, it is true, *tamassuks*, or bills of exchange on stamped paper, but they pay with more or less regularity, and know all the tricks of the trade; and even know, if necessary, how to spoil the wool by making a hole in it. They eat out of china, make use of silver plate, their abodes grow handsomer, are adorned with Lyons stuffs, with the finest upholstery, with mirrors, and their tables grant hospitality to the forbidden fruit, but their good faith loses on the one side what luxury and vanity gain on the other. And yet, notwithstanding the ravages of this foreign leprosy, the old dethroned commercial honour is still living; it is to be found amongst the old men, hoary with age, who have continued to be good Mussulmans, fanatical perhaps, but honest.

In fact, what part of our character is it that we Europeans allow to come to the surface and show itself to the eyes of these nations in our transactions with them? An immoderate love of lucre, which deserves in general a baser name. If they are acute, we are cunning; if they employ cunning, we have recourse to deceit . . . . Could we remain their equals in anything? Oh no! we are Christians; we must take the lead in everything, even in evil.

In Egypt, the inhabitants name (*Dhahab franghi*) gold of Europe, the jewels of a false standard, with which the country abounds. The compliment bears its moral lesson with it, and we must own that in many circumstances it is not usurped.

It would not be necessary to go far in order to find amongst the Christian houses, native and others, fortunes of a comparatively recent date, of which the source would not bear examination. These houses would be seen to be mixed up in foul dealings with the Custom-house, which put into their coffers customs dues which have not been paid: these houses have engaged themselves in operations with coin of foreign, and even Eastern fabrication, in dubious transactions, which, better than others, bring out in relief the *naïve* good faith of the Mussulmans. In short, at their base, gigantic tricks might be discovered, which the novelists of real life would lay hold of eagerly for sensational chapters.

In 1858, two Frenchmen were taken up in London, at the request of the Ottoman Government, and convicted of coining false Turkish money: a third culprit, the chief of them, a man who bore a great name and had occupied an honourable position in Egypt, succeeded in crossing the Straits before the visit of the police. The investigation of this affair revealed that a capital of several hundred thousand francs was to be furnished *by a great Paris house, in prepared gold*, for secretly coining Turkish pounds in England; the coiners provided themselves with copper on the spot for fabricating small change. At Alexandria, as was stated in a letter forming part of the case, Turkish piastres had been clandestinely struck for a long time; and what is remarkable is, that at the same time a Greek merchant of Manchester was arrested, at the complaint of the Ottoman Embassy, for having caused Ottoman money to be struck at Birmingham, which he exported to the Levant by the *barrel.*

This is in what the industrious operations of the French company were principally to consist. The Porte was at that time withdrawing from circulation some old coins, with a large proportion of alloy, which in moments of crisis had received a fictitious value, comparatively very high. This bullion returned to the treasury at a conventional rate much above its intrinsic value—in some cases the double. The margin, therefore, was attractive to the coiners, who had had dies engraved in London, which imitated the coins withdrawn from the currency in all their defects and imperfections; after that they succeeded admirably in making them old, by the aid of a corrosive liquid. A beshlik, or five piastres, cost these *merchants* a little less than two piastres; an altmishlik, or one piastre and a half, about a piastre; and so on.

Let us quote a few other examples out of a thousand. We will keep back the places and dates, and will only mention the facts. To fleece a Turk at the cost of his skin is a practice allowed by the worshippers of the dollar; it is the rule and the law. Whoever does not follow it is a fool. And then each one keeps as much as he can within the lame clauses of the Code . . . of what is possible. In England and the United States, where the blacklegs of trade have raised *close shaving* and *sharp practice* to a science, the acts which we relate would evidently pass for Arabian tales. Truth may sometimes appear improbable.

The government of a large province or pashalik produced a certain manufactured article, of general use. B., the vekil or overseer set over this branch of the public revenue, had a friend C., a famous merchant and a native Christian. C. asked B., Have you manufactured much this year? Between ourselves, the article is sought for; be discreet. When you have got heaps of goods ready, get your master to sell, and give me notice; I will be the buyer, and we shall understand one another." This advice is accepted and acted upon. The conversation then changes its scene, and continues in this wise:—B. says to the Governor, "Our warehouses are full, the treasury is empty, the moment is favourable; let us sell and replace the goods." The Governor: "Are you convinced of it? Very well! you have full leave." Exit the vekil. Last scene. C. having received notice: "I buy the whole in a mass at the price of yesterday, and pay at once a large sum on account to the treasury. How many pieces? 500,000? Very good. Do not announce the sale before twenty-four hours, and when the bazar presents itself say, 'Too late for this season, my lambs; come back next year, and we shall see about it: everything has been sold.' They will then be obliged to come to me. I will keep the price well up, and we will see one another afterwards."

The bazar sometimes bought at one or two francs' profit on each piece, and this game was renewed each year. The actors were in too high a position for the complaints of the timid public to reach the ears that were interested in hearing them. However, a day arrived when the master, more suspicious or better informed, demanded the accounts from the overseer, who then disappeared. The fortunate merchant, a Christian not under protection, would find the atmosphere heavy, and the sun burning to his eyes. He would hide by day and travel by night, until a ship took him away in quest of a Russian or Chinese passport; with the assistance of which, in returning to his country, he preserved his position, and added a padlock to his well-filled coffers. It will, perhaps, be objected, But why does the Mussulman vekil become the accomplice of the Christian merchant? We refer these wise critics to the serpent and the apple of the garden of Eden. Do not receivers make thieves?

On another occasion it is *Filan*,* a protected subject—of England, let us say—who, trusting to established usages, exported a prepared or manufactured article under the name of raw material—thanks to a certain conventional mark. The prepared goods were worth 200 piastres; the raw material, 90. The export dues were 12 per cent ad valorem, and the quantities exported enormous. An opinion may be formed of the importance of this illicit gain, weighing equally upon the treasury and the honest exporter.

Other skilful practitioners, Europeans let us say, so as to generalise their nationalities, used to sell to the Government . . . colossal lanterns, impossible cannons, first-rate frigates going twenty knots an hour, the proof *after* the letter. These masterpieces having been delivered, there was some delay before sending in the accounts, of which the profits alone would have sufficed to pay the Greek loan! Then came the quarter of an hour of Rabelais: the Government cried out . . . protested . . . when the *Deus ex machinâ* intervened, with a consular hat on his head, and the treasury paid up. All the wheels having been well greased, the noise ceased, leaving each one satisfied,

* Such a one.

even the injured party, for worse might often happen to it, in the shape of diplomatic complications! How many trains of artillery, how many bridges, how many whole arsenals, how many railways, what mountains of furniture and of coal, almost a fraction of England, have not been swallowed up—and paid for—without complaint, by this excellent pashalik! The bottom of the sea from Rhodes to the Bosphorus would literally be paved with these goods. We will say with the fabulist, I leave aside even better things than these! We will willingly join with the common sense of the public, which is already asking, "But why was the Government so simple?"* Caprice and flattery lead to the tree where perches the crow, and at the foot of which the large family of foxes permanently promenade themselves. The first will always be delighted to hear himself called the phœnix of the dwellers in these woods, and the cheeses which fall into the mouth of the second are always worth a lesson which is never turned to account. Has the commercial world in England forgotten the remonstrances which the Liverpool houses addressed

* The Government was not altogether simple; these abuses were owing to the pressure put upon the Government by Consuls, whom it had to keep satisfied for peace sake. One Consul in Egypt bought two houses cheap to sell them dear to Said Pasha. Other Consuls, or their relations, obtained orders for goods, locomotives, &c., which were highly remunerative and amounted to bribes, or black mail levied by the Consuls.—*Translator.*

on several occasions to the Foreign Office, on the subject of numerous cargoes of cotton, fraudulently exported from the Levant, without payment of the duty of 12 per cent ad valorem, and which were sold in the above-mentioned town at prices which were ruinous to the honest importers? The affair is too recent to have escaped the memory of the victims of those culpable operations, which gave a very undesirable notoriety to Christian houses of the first rank.

In reflecting on the unusual character of the facts which we have just related, and which have been taken at hazard from amidst hundreds of the same kind, this question naturally presents itself: How is it that these different Governments allowed themselves to be thus cheated, without seeking to cut at the root of the evil? To us Europeans, indeed, the remedy seems at first sight within easy reach, notwithstanding that the old continent is full of abuses and rotten institutions, from which it has great difficulty in freeing itself.

In the Levant it is still less easy. Everything seems to conspire in favour of these frauds. The administrative machine is complicated. *Red-tape* flourishes in all its splendour. There a day may be passed in a public office in running from one room to another, without any other result than a series of seals placed by a sort of automatons upon a sheet of paper. The office clerks are numerous, under-paid, and their salaries generally more or less in arrear. Their families are in a similar condition; people must live, and bakshish, when it knocks at the door of the official, is all the more alluring since these scribes, who are well aware of the ways of the world, say to themselves with some sort of reason, There is no great sin in gathering the crumbs fallen from the table of this rich merchant, who sits down without ceremony at that of our master. Little by little, abuse, at first shamefaced and solitary, became general. Now it forms almost the rule in the minds of those who know the value of their signature, and who have an intuition of the dubious character of the transaction, the papers of which are submitted to them in order that they may affix to it the "Open sesame" required by the treasury.

Let us suppose the case of a supply of cartridges, furnished by a European merchant to the Porte. If, instead of 2,000,000, only half has been consigned, and that notwithstanding this error a receipt has been taken for the whole, as is customary enough in those parts; if, in order to obtain this document, a certain weight has had to be placed in the pocket of him who has signed the precious document; if, in short, a fox is in the path prowling round the house, it will readily be understood what a feverish haste the contractor must experience who has already discounted in presents a part of his profits. Another example: A. has delivered cannons to the Government, which commission he has received without being limited as to the cost; he wants to gain as much as possible—two hundred per cent if he can, but he must avoid the rock of fixing a price higher or lower than that invoiced by B., another contractor of the same calibre. A. goes to look for X., the comptroller of accounts, who, for the sake of value received in proportion to the service rendered, produces the wished-for document. The figures are then neatly brought forward to a level, and in this way the Porte has the immense advantage of being served at a fixed price. From the lowest to the highest each functionary knows the motives for the anxiety of the vendor, and gets his work paid for according to its deserts. The hardest nut to crack is, without contradiction, the last. The comptroller, this king in his department, has his speech of gold and gestures of brass; he looks, and speaks little; he waits, and listens. Two words are enough for him; as soon as they have *sounded*, the "*sta bene*" is given.

In Egypt, book-keeping, the revision of accounts, fiscal administration in short, is in a great measure in the hands of native Christians, whose aptitude in all respects makes them fit for this kind of work. These scribes, or *Mahlems*, have a remarkable skill in all that pertains to accounts; they could teach some of the cleverest in that branch in Europe. Their memory is admirable, nothing escapes them; and the system which forms the basis of their capabilities is so complicated that it renders them indispensable: without them, it is impossible to understand anything of it. It is in these hundreds of books, of pages, and written folios, that lies the secret of their power. "Before having that scoundrel hanged," said a Pasha, "he must give in his accounts; and as he will never bring them to a close, his life is safe."

It is grievous, as may be seen, that the Mussulmans have not yet formed themselves to a profession which would give them insight into their own affairs.* The country would see its advantages in it, and the razzias practised upon the public treasury would, by degrees, be reduced to more presentable figures. There is a great objection to the employment of only certain individualities, belonging to another creed than that of the State, in an administration which, in addition to special talents, requires a great responsibility. Whenever these men are found in default,

---

* This applies more to the Cairo than to the Constantinople financial offices.— *Translator.*

they infallibly have some protection or other to invoke. Sometimes they may be compelled to make restitution; but for the most part the guilty pass without wetting themselves between the large drops of the shower, and the evil continues.

At Constantinople it is the Armenians who, more or less, hold in their hands the thousand threads of finance. That nation has furnished its contingent of capacity in various branches. Banking and the dragomanship in Constantinople and Egypt have been the steps which have raised many of them to honours and fortune. The Armenians have the qualities and the faults of the Levantines.* At Constantinople they mint money, manufacture powder, farm the asphalt, and in general fish in waters where the largest fish are to be found. This nation is distinguished for its activity, its prudence, its aptitude for litigious matters,—the whole united to a certain affability which pleases and attracts.

As soon as the Osmanlys shall agree to live a little less as fine gentlemen, reforms will become easy, because, seeing things from a nearer point of view, they will be able to judge them better. As soon as appointments become more stable and better paid, as soon as they can be properly filled

* They are much superior to the Levantines; they have more domestic virtues, and less vanity.—*Translator.*

by instructed Mussulman subjects, protected or punished by equitable regulations, the administration will become honourable. Until then all other attempts at improvement will be useless, and will feel the effects of the *corrupt head* of the Greek proverb.

It will not require a long time for these populations to arrive at the required degree of maturity, for they are intelligent, and form themselves and learn very readily. Reforms in this direction have already begun in Egypt, where the education of the masses is more advanced, and begins to produce good results. The great leprosy which gnaws at the Empire has always been seated in the ignorance of the people, for whom reading and writing were formerly unusual talents. No newspapers, few books, no literature to instruct and raise the nation to a sense of its own dignity. History was a sealed book, and when war brought misery and humiliation upon the country, the people hardly troubled itself to ascertain the causes. In its eyes the all-powerful Sultans represented science, and fatality explained the rest. As in the last century, Voltaire and his disciples were infallibly quoted as the source of all ills, so the influence of Christendom was for them the universal cause, to the account of which taxes and requisitions were set down. Thence that inbred suspicion, those instincts of revenge, of enmity, which have always been assumed to be the necessary consequences of differences of religion. Thence that feeling of discomfort which still exists virtually in the relations of the Mussulmans with the Christians, and which sometimes lead them to act summarily towards them. They (the Mussulmans) thus put the wrong on their side, whilst in the outset the rights of the case, and an amount of reflection and patience, would have made them gain their cause.

But there is another cause to be assigned for the difficulties amidst which the Empire struggles, although these may be considered as being singularly diminished, if not on the eve of giving place to a more normal and prosperous state of things. This cause lies in the comparatively vicious representation of the powers in relation with the Sublime Porte.

The greater number of European Envoys are sent to Constantinople, either to favour and promote a policy hostile to Turkey, or to make only a brief residence at the seat of a government of which they know neither the habits nor the susceptibilities. A few of them, better informed respecting the men and the affairs of the country, are not free in their action, and are under the necessity of submitting to certain instructions, tending to prevent them from openly counteracting their colleagues in a policy which is feared, or which seems necessary. With the aid of the intrigues and proximity of Russia, Constantinople is, on that very account, the point where the spirit of strife has heaped up the greatest amount of inflammable and explosive materials. A rather hasty word causes the fleets and armies of Christendom to converge there. A military tune, beaten with the finger-ends upon the ministerial window-panes in Downing Street, reproduces itself in cannon-shot on the shores of the Bosphorus.

Notwithstanding these truths, which are known to all the Courts, the old system still prevails. England and Austria alone seem to have understood, that when the fittest man has been found for a post he should be left in it as long as possible, so that the experience which he has obtained of the affairs of the country may not be lost to everybody when he changes his residence. It is certain that the act of accrediting an ambassador to a court does not of itself necessarily imply a friendly understanding or conformity of political views; but our observations upon the spirit which, with a few honourable exceptions, animates the diplomatic body at Constantinople, however novel they may appear to the antagonists of the Porte, are none the less borne out by facts. The Envoys arrive at their posts as they would at the camp of a hostile general, who cannot be attacked on the field of battle, and whom they seek to conquer in detail by a system of opposition in a manner instinctive, if it is not the result of higher instructions.*

We do not hesitate to assert, that so long as this kind of odious routine exists the difficulties which we have mentioned will remain as an insurmountable obstacle in the path of the reforms which people seem to wish to impose upon Turkey, without giving her the time to set about them by her own means.

As a contrast to this picture, let us render a just

* Another usage, not conducive to harmonious relations between the Porte and the foreign representatives, is the custom of employing dragomans for their communications; the motives for this custom are obsolete, since every Turkish foreign minister will be henceforward, and has been for many years, as conversant with the French language as the foreign representatives: and it is time that this custom should fall into disuse. It is disadvantageous to both parties. The European governments cannot be so well served by Levantines related to others in the service of a rival government, as by their own accredited agents. The dragomans form a confederation, whose interest is to create business to magnify their own importance: they go daily to the public offices with or without business, and waste much of their own and of other people's time. As a class they are ill-educated, Levantine in feelings and opinions, neither showing any fitting respect to the Turkish ministers, nor susceptible of being respected by them.—*Translator.*

tribute of praise to the minister, pre-eminent amongst the honest men who are an honour to Great Britain, and who has represented her in the Levant during a long and brilliant period. Lord Stratford Canning may be quoted here in support of the English maxim, " The right man in the right place." A stranger to the pettifogging of the chanceries, of which Constantinople has always been the theatre,* having no other care nor other flag than his duty, he combined the exercise of it by indicating to the Porte the road to prosperity. Nevertheless, without neglecting the interests of the Queen, Lord Stratford was the sincere friend of Turkey— the only one, it may be said; because, with private inclinations which led him not to counteract what in his conscience he believed to be the good of that country, he represented, with a perfect rectitude of judgment and a remarkable dignity, the frank and honest side of English policy. He was always to be met at the head of those attempts at improvement which must place Turkey in the rank which the Treaty of Paris has assigned to her. He advised and sustained the cabinets and the men who were true friends of progress—of that slow and solid progress which founds and consolidates states. All his efforts tended to the restor-

* If there is any drawback to this statement, it has been owing to the dragoman system.—*Translator.*

ation of the dignity, and to the integrity of the Ottoman Empire. We need not say that he had as a natural antagonist the Representative of Russia, whom the French Ambassador sometimes seconded, if not from identity with the views of the Muscovite Cabinet, at least from the feelings of an old national rivalry. It was in the midst of this noble struggle of every day, and after a most honourable career, that the English Ministry appointed a successor to this veteran of diplomacy; and that, not on account of any conflict of opinion between the Queen's Government and her Ambassador, but rather as a spontaneous act of generous deference to the susceptibilities of a power which had just received so severe a lesson.

We will not terminate this part of our work without recalling to mind, that the project of Lord Stratford's predilection was the gradual transformation of the capitulations, which still regulate the mode of life of European Christians in the Levant, and to substitute for them an ampler wording, more compatible with the national dignity, without taking away from them any of the safeguards necessary to the security of good and honest men. His Lordship knew, that the robberies and assassinations almost daily committed in Constantinople and at Smyrna had for their authors Christians, most of whom were subjected to his jurisdiction, Maltese, Ionians, &c.; but he understood very well, that the capitulations themselves are not only a brevet of impunity for incorrigible malefactors, but also that they give to the Mussulman inhabitants of the country a very sorry opinion of the impartiality and of the retributive justice of the Christian powers. Moreover, this Ambassador attempted on several occasions to come to an understanding with his colleagues, in order to bring about a provisional revision of the clauses, until such time as the modified measures might become official and have the force of law. But he never succeeded. His efforts were constantly shattered against the Muscovite *non possumus*, or the absence of special instructions on the part of the other representatives. Thanks to this regrettable policy, the Mussulman population continues to enjoy the edifying spectacle afforded to them by thieves and assassins walking about free as air, from Buyukdereh to Pera; their pockets filled with plunder, and a bloody dagger in their belt; and in broad day pursuing, even into the coffee-houses, the victims of their audacity! If a rayah robs a European of a single para, there are not guards enough to lay hands upon him, or law enough to punish him: the rope or a drowning in the Bosphorus seem to be the only punishments capable of satisfying the injured party. Two steps further on a *tchapkun* (vagabond), a European or protected Christian, murders in a coffee-house, robs, or abandons his victim without plundering him, as the case may be, goes out, and returns home as quietly as would a priest going to say mass. And if the local police interferes, purely and simply for the sake of order, and arrests for the honour of the foreign flag this scum of the Christian community, there is a general uproar, an appeal to the capitulations and the reserved rights! as if there were any for these outcasts of humanity! The goings and comings of the dragomans of the Embassies only cease when *these unhappy victims of Mussulman oppression* can freely give themselves up to the pleasures of the promenade, and enjoy without obstacle the song of the nightingales which charm the shores of the Bosphorus. These examples of our spirit of equity do not belong to ancient history; they are given every day at Cairo, at Alexandria, at Smyrna, as well as at the capital—everywhere, in short, where the Christian element is sufficiently numerous to cause such anomalies to be accepted.

We will take a fresh proof from civil life. The Porte has liberally and wisely granted to Europeans the right of acquiring real property throughout the Empire, under the very reasonable condition for the proprietors of submitting themselves to the edicts which regulate the taxes, as well as to the municipal obligations which are derived from them. Up to this time, however, the law has been eluded. Houses and land have become the property of Europeans, without these having ever contributed anything towards the State taxes, either for keeping up the streets, the roads, the watercourses, or for the maintenance of the local police. The Porte urges its claims: capitulations freely granted are brought up against it, and as the Government has its hands overloaded with more important affairs, this question has gone to join a number of others, more or less similar, the solution of which is postponed, through diplomatic apathy, until the Greek Kalends.*

We think that we have amply proved that Christendom, taken individually or as a whole,

* England, more than any other European power, seems to be precluded from asking for its subjects the right to hold land in Turkey, since English law does not allow foreigners to hold real property in England—very naturally, since the landholder in England enjoys various civil and political rights. Under the capitulations, the acquisition of real property by foreigners in Turkey is far more detrimental to Turkey than an infraction of the English law could be in England.

Vattel, liv. ii. chap. vii. sect. 114.—" Tout état est le maître d'accorder ou de refuser aux étrangers la faculté de posséder des terres ou d'autres biens immeubles dans son territoire. S'il la leur accorde, ces biens étrangers demeurent soumis à la jurisdiction et

whether belonging to the commercial or to the political world, has not exactly preached the morality of modern civilisation by its example to the Mussulmans. It has, on the contrary, according to our view, done everything to destroy the respect and esteem for that which power, right, and a certain *prestige*, had gained for it in more ancient times.

But this is not all. We have just unveiled one of the bad sides of the treaties, that one which keeps up bitter feelings in the minds of the Mussulmans; we have passed in review the vices of Christendom, a hundred times worse than those of Islamism. We have rapidly portrayed the ways and usages of the mercantile class—of that class which devotes itself to that industry, of such multifarious branches, which Napoleon wittily called "organised brigandage." We will now pass on to another category of that European society, whose excep-

aux lois du pays, sujets aux taxes comme les autres. L'empire du souverain s'étend dans tout le territoire, et il serait absurde d'en excepter quelques parties par la raison qu'elles sont possédées par des étrangers. Si le souverain ne permet point aux étrangers de posséder des immeubles, personne n'est en droit de s'en plaindre; car il peut avoir de très-bonnes raisons d'en user ainsi; et les étrangers ne pouvant s'attribuer aucun droit dans son territoire, ils ne doivent pas même trouver mauvais qu'il use de son pouvoir et de ses droits de la manière qu'il croit la plus salutaire à l'état. Et puisque le souverain peut refuser aux étrangers la faculté de posséder des immeubles, il est le maître sans doute de ne l'accorder qu'à certaines conditions."—*Translator.*

tional functions put them so much the more in view, since they belong to a higher class.

The Consular body, so honourable everywhere else, in general falls more than behind-hand with what is expected in the ports of the Levant. Nobody doubts the good intentions of the Governments represented at Constantinople, nor their desire to have honest Consuls, protecting and punishing, administering and acting, with as much dignity as disinterestedness, according to law and justice. With regard to this there is but one voice and one opinion. How, then, does it come to pass that some of these subaltern agents, for the most part depending upon the Ambassadors at Constantinople, allow themselves reprehensible actions, which are censured strongly by the public, without bringing down upon themselves the chastisement which official control, careful of the commonest decency, could not fail to inflict upon them?* It would be well, how-

---

* It is difficult to find any answer to this question; but this indifference, however culpable, will be understood better from the fact, that in addition to the numerous Consuls who have unfitted themselves for their posts, one could be named who continues to be employed after the Government was aware that it had been defrauded by him. If Her Majesty's Government could pass this over, what misconduct would not meet with impunity? An opinion may be formed from this example with respect to other European Governments and Consuls in Turkey.—*Translator.*

ever, for once to show the Mussulmans that Christian justice and protection are not matters of traffic.

We will be very brief upon the subject of Consul-generals, Consuls, and subaltern agents occupied in trade. The inconvenience of that incompatibility is glaring: a man may naturally be drawn on to take, without intending it, the law into his own hands, to employ his influence and immunities here and there for his own benefit. From the affairs which these functionaries do not always deal with in conformity to the strict usage of the country, there arise from time to time conflicts between the Government and the consular agent, in a matter in which the latter is both judge and pleader. It is especially in the lower part of the corps, the consular agents and sub-agents in the interior, that the evil shows itself in all its force. At Damietta, for instance, there is a Levantine bent down under the weight of consular dignities; he represents at third hand fifteen or sixteen nations. The public offices are continually besieged by the claims of this hundred-headed *diplomat*, who, in addition to his innumerable functions, finds time to be one of the well-to-do merchants of the place.

We will examine more particularly the subject of protections extended to Christian and Jewish rayahs, sometimes bestowed gratuitously, but for the most part sold for ready money.* Properly speaking, there is no tariff established for the regulation of these equivocal transactions; an arrangement is made as to presents, and the sums thus paid are far from being inconsiderable. In time they make up very handsome fortunes for the unscrupulous practisers of this consular trade, which transforms into Christian subjects individuals wearing turbans, long robes, and possessing only their own mother-tongue, Turkish or Arabic, in which to congratulate their adopted Sovereign when on his travels. Such a medley of subjects of different nationalities can hardly be imagined: a human mosaic which is not without originality, in Egypt for instance, when it presents itself to the inspection of some prince eager for new impressions, when he is received at an audience by the Viceroy during his tour in the Levant, and he finds himself surrounded by a crowd of his *countrymen* in turbans, riding on donkeys like true sons of Egypt or of Israel, which they are.

* A Levantine, a British Vice-Consul at Mytilene, used to take his consular seal with him *after dinner*, and manufacture Ionian subjects at the café: these were disfranchised by the polished and learned scholar who held the consulship at a later period. It is a pity that this gentleman is not sent on a tour of revision through the consulates of the Levant, combining antiquarian research with the purging of those Augean stables. — *Translator.*

It is known that the firmans of the capitulations grant to the foreign representatives the right of extending the immunities of the national privileges to all the rayahs employed in their official and private residence, which, in virtue of the principle of ex-territoriality, is considered as a part of the country accredited. The number of these persons employed is laid down in the treaties, and if it is exceeded in moderation, the local government can shut its eyes upon an irregularity which has no further inconvenience. But when, under any pretext, a Consul arbitrarily extends his protection to the inhabitants, on whatever grounds it may be, beyond the prescribed limits, in order to withdraw these individuals from the action of their natural authorities, when this international offence is accompanied by the very aggravating circumstance of remuneration, which converts it into a traffic, then the scandal has reached its summit, and to allow it to endure is a weakness, a crime which it is necessary to punish.*

* In Siam, a foreign Consul had a number of abusive subjects; in addition to this he sold spirit-licenses at a low rate: in doing this he not only undersold the Siamese Government, but did much harm by increasing the number of spirit-shops, which it was the object of the high price required by the Siamese Government for a license to check. — *Translator.*

The Russian consular agents devote themselves much to the industry of protection. Cairo and Alexandria abounded, before the Italian war, in artificial subjects of the King of Naples and the Grand Duke of Tuscany. Prussia seems to have in the Levant a rather large number of subjects, of Turkish, Arabic, and Armenian speech. The flags which respect themselves the most are those of France and Spain. The others are not particularly notorious in this respect. These deplorable proceedings showed themselves in all their cynicism during the Crimean war; when Abbas Pasha, upon orders received from Constantinople, had to send away all the Hellenic subjects from the Egyptian territory. To the great surprise of the Viceroy, a great number of these, as if by enchantment, were found to be European protected subjects, and claimed what they called their political rights; and conflicts of authority ensued, which, fortunately, were not serious.

Temporary protections gratuitously given may have been justifiable in a period of great calamities, and at a time when religious animosities existed in all their force. But at the present time there is no longer any reason for their existence, cruelties and exactions by the Porte having long since happily been left behind, amongst the things of the past. The motive of the abuses which we denounce does not consist therefore, in consular philanthropy, stimulated by the active solicitude of Christendom. It must be sought for elsewhere. It will be found in the decided taste of the non-Mussulman rayahs for shaking off any yoke placed over their equivocal proceedings; in the extraordinary seduction offered by operations made with the Government, and which, when it discovered the numberless frauds of which it was the victim, it would probably refuse to sanction, or to bring to the desired conclusion, if the parties who were to profit depended on its authority. In this case it would be necessary to submit to disagreeable investigations, the least consequence of which would be to reduce, if not to absorb the profits; besides, highly situated associates might be compromised, which would evidently spoil the trade. But when the party enjoys a European protection, no matter which, things take another aspect. Is there any hitch with the Custom-house, or with any office, there is a rush to the Consulate, which sends still faster a kavass or a dragoman, as the case may be, with the Consul's *compliments*, and the difference is arranged . . . at the expense of somebody, of course. If the affair is important, the Consul gets into his carriage, carries his compliments himself, writes, protests, threatens, goes into a flurry, and conquers by utter exhaustion . . . *casus belli* are always heavy clouds, of which people are glad to clear their horizon.

Let us mention another anomaly, not less glaring, created by the capitulations, and kept up by the various interests which it protects by implication, and one quite as fruitful in shocking abuses as the preceding ones. We mean the administration of justice in its different branches, with regard to the European community.

About seventeen powers are represented at Constantinople by seventeen ministers, who themselves are more or less represented by as many consuls-general, consuls, vice-consuls, and infinitesimal agents, posted from Trebizond to Smyrna, from Beyrout to Alexandria, from Cairo to Jiddah, from Suez to Damietta and Rosetta, &c. &c. If railways and electric telegraphs, those extended roots of the great tree of modern civilisation, have in some measure lowered the selfish barriers which formerly hindered the mutual relations between the states of Europe, human reason does not seem to have kept pace with locomotives and electric wires. Each state has carefully preserved its abuses, its usages, its language, and its laws; and the tower of Babel, instead of having fallen into ruin, still dominates over the East in its whole extent. Seventeen consulates, seventeen different jurisdictions, legislations, and administrations of justice! And what justice!* It is easy to understand that it is rather lame, whatever might be the good intentions of the judges.

What is the result of this official chaos? Let us examine briefly this difficult question. In the first place, in virtue of the principle of ex-territoriality, established by the capitulations, each Embassy, and so each Consulate, representing a portion of the country accredited, becomes in reality the legal *domicile* of the subjects whom it protects. Consequently, every plaintiff in any cause is obliged to accept the jurisdiction of the defendant. Now, an Englishman and a Russian, dwelling in the same port in the Levant, but at variance about a commercial difference, proceed to the settlement of it exactly as if one lived in Cumberland and the other at Tobolsk. In the second place, the consular courts, upon whose benches, for want of better, occasionally illiterate judges are called to sit, only pronounce

* A case of barratry occurred at Constantinople: three Perotes insured a ship at London, Marseilles, and Trieste, and instructed the captain to lose it: he sent them word that he had done so, but thought it more advantageous to sell the ship on the Barbary coast, so that the fraud was discovered, and the insurances, though claimed, were not lost to the insurance companies. But owing to the confusion of jurisdiction, the Perotes belonging to different nationalities, and being influential persons, no steps were taken against them. — *Translator.*

upon the first hearing, and appeals go to Constantinople, to be unravelled in the presence of the legations of the respective parties. In this last respect France alone is an exception to the rule. This power, whose excellent traditions in matter of jurisprudence are the honour of her magistracy, has from the first attributed to the Imperial Court of Aix the right of hearing and deciding all causes coming under this head, arising in the Levant. However this may be, it will be easy to understand how many reefs are set in the passages leading to a justice so costly, and so tedious and difficult to obtain; how much change of place it requires; and, in case the matter is entrusted to agents at Constantinople, by how slight a thread depends the gaining of an important suit!

In considering this active and heterogeneous community, whose operations are as extended as they are varied, and the interests so closely bound up with the financial state of Europe, the dangers of this constitutional vice will be at once perceived; and a just idea will be formed of the innumerable difficulties, the conflicts of jurisdiction, the means of avoiding a process, the dubious manœuvres, the quibbles, the denials of justice, which such a state of things necessarily carries in its train.

It has happened, in cases of bankruptcy, that

paid clerks, or relations of one of the chief creditors, himself a connexion of the bankrupt, have been named by the Consulate as liquidators or commissioners for the bankrupt's estate! The water of the stream went naturally to the river, leaving nothing wherewith to quench the thirst of the other claimants.*

By the side of what may be called this chronic anarchy there prospers a self-constituted bar, whose intelligent sagacity, more than University degrees, succeeds pretty well in making the best of the classic oyster. As the greater part of the causes brought before the consular courts belong to commercial matters, and these amateur lawyers almost all issue from the ranks of the mercantile community, their labour is very easy. It is all reduced for them to a knowledge of local customs, and to a suitable portion of common sense, in which they are not wanting. Moreover, a too-learned show of science sends the judges to sleep nearly everywhere; and would infallibly become a calamity in a country where the

---

* One of the chief vices of the consular jurisdiction is that impartiality on the part of the Consul, or of the assessors whom he sometimes nominates, in these small communities is almost impossible. Yet a recent correspondence in the newspapers congratulates the British residents at Smyrna on the fact of the newly-appointed British Consul being related by marriage to one of the chief Smyrna houses!—*Translator.*

mind and the body are kindly disposed to the *siesta.*

In criminal matters the consequences are still worse, if possible. The culprit usually passes between the thousand flaws in the formalities. As the consular jurisdiction only extends to civil, commercial, and police matters, the consular clerks in these cases confine themselves to preparing the case against the defendant; and both are sent to Europe, to the judges whom they concern. Nine times out of ten these dismiss the defendant, or the prisoner, either from a want of clearness in the accusation, or rather by reason of the nullities with which it abounds, or because the most necessary formalities have not been observed at the outset. A number of assassins, forgers, coiners, &c., escape thus from the action of the law, and are let loose upon the continent after a short detention.*

No doubt it is better to acquit a hundred guilty persons than to condemn one innocent one. We do not dispute the advantages of this excellent maxim; but it cannot be sufficient to perpetuate a system

---

* In June or July, 1864, two men were sent prisoners to Liverpool by one of Her Majesty's Consuls; as no indictment had arrived with them, from an accident of the Post-office or other cause, they had to be set at liberty, and probably departed to America.— *Translator.*

which by no means adds to the esteem which European Christendom ought to enjoy in the Levant.

* * * * *

Up to this time, Western industry has done hardly anything in the Levant worth mentioning. Here and there, as has been the case in Egypt, some enterprise has been got up, with the secret object of realising a large profit by making it over to the Government, and has not succeeded in bearing the fruit which the country had a right to expect from it. On the one side, the Ottoman Government has rather looked with an eye of suspicion upon the attempts of this kind made on different occasions by honourable European companies.* On the other, the Christian colony whose aspirations are directed towards the chances of large profits has little sympathy, or perhaps aptitude, for the industry which gains the pence of which are composed the shillings, which in time form the pounds. It requires other baits to draw its attention, and to lead it to employ its time and money in a branch of commerce which develops the riches of the country.

* * * * *

At Paris, in the unwholesome regions of a certain

---

* This has been caused by *fiascos*, such as the recent one of the Smyrna and Aidin Railway Company.— *Translator*.

titled and ruined woman of bad reputation, it was usual to project "campaigns" in Egypt, to raise the wind when fortune was at a low ebb by means of a razzia upon the Viceroy. These people used mutually to form wishes for each other to obtain commissions for furniture, for mirrors, for any kind of article, with millions of profit as the result, and perhaps also, by luck, a red ribbon . . . . for having encouraged commerce and art! The moral standard had fallen so low that gentlemen, bearers of fine names, used to arrive at Alexandria, provided, generally, with semi-official letters; they used to get introduced to His Highness by their representative, who solicited for those who were recommended to him a little drop of milk from that good cow, so much more adored than ever was the ancient Apis. The Viceroy, who did not know how to refuse, used to grant the favour sued for with contempt upon his lips. Could he act differently? The habit had been fallen into, and his Christian officials who were most intimate with him, those who seemed most devoted to him, pressed and worried him without ceasing, so as to win their share of the prey. The fortunate traveller used then to quit the palace, commissioned to supply thousands of tons of coal, of coke, cloth, or shoes for the army. Adroit associates under-bought the commissions for a large discount, and the Boulevard des Italiens in a short time was full of the success of the expedition.

* * * * *

The perpetual cry of a few greedy, and probably ill-paid Consuls, was invariably this:—"Highness, a little affair for my subject, for my *protégé*, if you please!" And orders for carriages, for rails, cannon, coal, floating batteries, &c. &c., fell thick as hail into the laced hats, which, like intelligent workshops, distilled the profits and brought them by hidden channels into the interested pockets.

One or two of these functionaries, for instance, arranged in such a manner as always to have a handful of equivocal lawsuits in their pockets, of which they let a corner peep out. With these from time to time they threatened the Pasha, with polite circumlocutions; he, wearied and worried by these continual assaults, sometimes made an end of it, addressing them in this wise:—"Gentlemen, you know better than I do that these manœuvres are most unworthy, and that your clients make us do a dirty business; but as it is repugnant to me to fight with cut-throats, here, take 100, 200, or 300,000 francs; make what arrangements you like, and leave me at peace."

To this painful sketch let us add one of the

most precious objects of the rich collection. It is said, that amongst the hyperbolical claims which appeared after the death of Said Pasha, there was a bill presented of 550,000 francs for *"fresh fruit"* supplied to His Highness, and behind which was naturally to be found the consular *Deus ex machinâ*. What imagination! and what an excessively relaxing diet!

We will end these very incomplete notes with an account of a regrettable occurrence, which happened a few days after the accession of the reigning Viceroy, and concerning which the French papers at the time made some noise. Impartial readers will see on which side lay the first fault, and they will compare the sensitive zeal which some Consuls always bring to the service of insulted *national honour*, with the servile fuss which they sometimes employ to satisfy the scandalous appetites of their subordinates.

A Frenchman, belonging to the Suez Canal, was passing on horseback through one of the most populous quarters of the Turkish part of Alexandria; there was a crowd in the bazar, and soldiers were hurrying through in great numbers so as to fill up the road, which was covered with mud and puddles. The rider, finding himself delayed in his progress, and being, no doubt, in a hurry to arrive, attempted to force his way, by hastening the pace of his horse, which caused a confusion among the passers-by, some of whom complained of having been hustled and splashed. Hands were lifted to the horse's head and stopped it short. This proceeding seems to have exasperated the rider, who apostrophised the soldiers, and mixed with the epithets which he bestowed upon them the word *Khanzir* (pig), the grossest insult which a Christian can throw in the face of a Mussulman. The rest may be guessed. The crowd, excited by the death of the Pasha and the accession of his successor, was anything but disposed to be indulgent. The rider was, very unfortunately, unhorsed and ill-treated, and laid a complaint before the Consul-general. This functionary, forgetting, no doubt, that the new Viceroy was a member of the family of Mehemet Ali, of the man who had always shown himself just and equitable towards the Christians, who had made the greatest number of spontaneous concessions to their usages, an example nobly followed by his successors,—this functionary, in short, acts towards H. H. Ismail Pasha as summarily, not to say more, as if he had had to deal with the commander of a body of Tae-pings in China. He imperiously exacted an "immediate" reparation, without admitting the slightest previous inquiry, and setting aside the action of the tribunals of the country. He put the knife to the Viceroy's throat, and inflicted a humiliation upon him which Christians and Mussulmans felt perfectly, especially as His Highness had never refused to give satisfaction.

Is it thus that the matter would have been treated elsewhere—in France, at Paris, for instance, where the municipal police, less scrupulous as to formalities than is generally believed, "seizes" brutally, under the slightest pretext, passengers who walk or ride, and whose demeanour, more than pacific, contrasts with the Gallic excitableness abroad?* Why obtain redress by such means, and so cast a slur upon the justice of a Government which not only has always granted it, but which has constantly gone to meet the most minute exigencies: whilst, on the other hand, it is honoured so far as to pocket its money, and to lie down at its feet to beg its favours? Why offer it so deadly an affront in the sight of the country, and trample under foot an old friendship and honourable antecedents, full of a hospitality which is nowhere else to be met with as ample or as generous? It must be confessed, the flag of Christendom, formerly so pure and resplendent in the Levant, is now dragged down by a

---

* After the "Italian plot" of the spring of 1864, the police took up several persons in the Bois de Boulogne, merely because their personal appearance was suspicious.—*Translator.*

weight of indignity and baseness which the floods of noble blood shed in the Crusades will never wash away.

In Egypt, when the wind blows from the quarter of law-suits, that *Khamsin* of the Viceroys, the storm carries all before it. Nothing protects the treasury from it, whose coffers seem like fragile card-houses. For ten justifiable suits, there are forty which are lame and fifty dishonest. They are brought on upon all and every occasion. They are the subject of dreams, and are planned beforehand, whilst soliciting the Viceroy for concessions, whose terms, framed with cunning ambiguity, place the Government at a later date under the alternative of buying back, at the cost of millions, the unlucky favour, or of confiding the claims arising out of it to the honour of arbitrators, who have much talent but not always enough of conscience; who sometimes take with both hands, and infallibly condemn the richest of the pleaders. There have been exceptions to this rule, but they have been very rare. Said Pasha has left behind him a few thorns of this kind, the extraction of which will be no easy matter, especially if the established system continues to be the same. The treasury has only to take good care of itself, the guests are numerous, and their appetites sharpened.

In fact, nothing is easier than the attack, and nothing more problematical than the defence. There is always a sufficiently large number of Consuls-general, real rifled artillery, ready to back the suits which their subjects bring against the Viceroy. The lawyers begin the siege; by the aid of intrigues and Latin quotations the affair soon becomes so confused that the Government, no longer comprehending it, may be effectually frightened. Then menaces intervene, and, if need be, arbitrators — commissioners *pro formâ;* and the curtain falls upon the "execution" of the Treasury, the victim designated beforehand, and always sacrificed.*

It is evident, a hundred times evident, that a state of things so monstrously unjust, so abominably immoral and tyrannical, cannot be prolonged any length of time. The honour and the interests of Egypt require a change, both radical and prompt. Let the Viceroy adopt for all that concerns his government, with the reservations and the modifications required by the civil and religious condition of the country, the code of a progressive and intelli-

* This has been borne out by the large indemnity obtained by the Suez Canal Company for yielding up the concessions of land made by the late Said Pasha in opposition to the fundamental laws of the empire.—*Translator.*

gent European power—that of Belgium, for instance. And if there are but ten just men in Egypt, it will be more than are wanted to decide upon the merits of the actions brought against the Government. In the contrary case, it would not be difficult for the Viceroy to come to an understanding with the Ministry of His Majesty King Leopold upon the subject of an official or private arrangement, authorising a High Belgian Court to lend him the assistance of its lights and services. This measure, or such another having the same result, would arrest, as if by enchantment, the torrential flow of lawsuits. Dishonest suits would die of a natural death, leaving honest and really well-founded causes to their ordinary course.

Then the function of the Consuls would again become what it should never have ceased to be. These officials would represent their Government with regard to their veritable subjects, within the limits of justice and equity, without overstepping those of a well-defined jurisdiction. They would no longer support the claims of their subjects for the sake of a shameful per-centage, and by methods which the laws of the country which has accredited them would never sanction. They would no longer become the "commission agents" of operations more or less above-board, for the sake of a present, or a portion of the illicit profits. In this manner they would recover the sentiment of their own dignity, and by degrees would shake off that humiliating dust with which their cloth has been covered by culpable complaisance and an unavowable thirst for gain.

The European Governments, on their side, would make better appointments, and would give better pay to their agents in Egypt, where living is expensive, where temptations are numerous, and where luxury is carried to an excess which surpasses all notions of what is absurd.

Lastly, the local Government would cease to see, in certain members of this body, either adversaries or friends, according to the scale of favours which it granted or suffered to be extorted from it. It would respect those who know how to cause themselves to be respected; and if a good hint or good advice came from Europe, it would be received without suspicion—with gratitude even, from an intermediary who no longer sells his services, nor begs for favours for rapacious and dishonest solicitors.

III.

THE EFFECTS OF CONTEMPT FOR INTERNATIONAL LAW.

" Justitia non nostra constitutio, sed divina lex, et vinculum societatis humanæ. In hac non est quod æstimemus quid expediat, expedit tibi quicquid illa dictaverit. Quisquis ergo hanc sectari desideras, Deum time prius et ama, ut ameris a Deo. Amabilis eris Deo, si in hoc illum imitaberis, ut velis omnibus prodesse et nulli nocere."—*SENECA*.

IN the middle ages the name of Religion served as the plea and justification of aggression upon weaker nations; it led to their spoliation and enslavement. The Pope, then the head of all Christendom, partitioned Asia and America amongst the Christian Princes. Spain took the lead in these expeditions, so contrary to all the principles of justice and international law; and members of the Spanish Government were also the first to protest against the acts of tyranny and injustice into which the Colonists were led by natural steps, deriving from their unlawful invasion of unoffending countries.*

The nineteenth century, which professes to have discarded fanaticism, has substituted the advance of civilisation for the extension of Christianity as its pass-word. Humanity has not gained by the change; aggressions continue as before, in defiance of international law: the motive in the present time is more undisguisedly selfish, since modern aggressions are made under the pretext of commerce, by which the aggressors hope to enrich themselves: the absence of a religious element, however mistaken it may have been, makes itself felt, since there is now no one to plead for the vanquished. The exception to this in modern times is in New Zealand, where deserving members of the Church of England have interested themselves in the fate of the New Zealanders, and have not ceased to protest against the spoliation and extermination going on in that unhappy land.

* "In 1542 the Bishop Las Casas presented a memorial to Charles V., remonstrating against enslaving the Peruvians. He maintained that if the Indians, as it was pretended, would not labour unless compelled, the white man would still find it for his interest to cultivate the soil; and that if he should not be able to do so, that circumstance would give him no right over the Indian, since *God does not allow evil that good may come of it.* This lofty morality, it will be remembered, was from the lips of a Dominican in the sixteenth century."—*Prescott's* "*Conquest of Peru,*" book iv. chap. vii.

Japan has been subjected to the two forms under which European aggression has presented itself, in the sixteenth century and in our days. Let comparison be made between these two periods of intercourse with Japan. In the sixteenth century, the Europeans made numerous proselytes, and gained a great influence over the councils of that state; their abuse of that influence led to their expulsion. In the nineteenth century, the Europeans have no sooner arrived than they excite universal hostility on the part of the Japanese, and the desire to be rid of the unwelcome intruders. Yet it is said, with much show of reason, that Japan has remained comparatively stationary since the first visit of Europeans, whilst Europe has greatly advanced. But such superior civilisation should more readily obtain admiration and a favourable reception, than that of the sixteenth century. Why is it not so? Perhaps the improvement of the nineteenth century is only material, and there is a falling off in the respect felt for legality and the rights of others. Certainly, among the British visitors to Japan in the nineteenth century, there have not been many persons so respectable as Mr. W. Adams, the English pilot, or master, in the beginning of the sixteenth century.*

* " The lowly-born William Adams, when cast in wretchedness on the shores of Japan, was not indeed received as a prince; yet this

But the people of the present time cannot justify themselves by what took place in the sixteenth century, with respect to their conduct towards other nations; for since then the duties of nations *towards their neighbour* have been codified, and form international law, which has become fixed; but is not on that account more regarded: and as these laws are the expression of justice and order, the disregard of them is the cause of many of the evils from which we suffer.

In the sixteenth century Europe was a prey to wars of religion, which had been made the pretext for wars of aggrandisement and rapine. This state of disorder caused Suarez, and after him Grotius, Vattel, and others, to write those works which have become international law. These writings did not become law from any authority of the authors, neither were they subsequently formally accepted as such: but their weight and authority consist in this, that their authors sought out and laid down the first principles of right and justice, which stand and re-

man, commencing life in the capacity of "apprentice to Master Nicolas Diggines, of Limehouse," eventually attained rank and acquired possession in the Empire equal to those of a prince. With no claims to consideration but talent and good conduct, he became the esteemed councillor of the sagacious and powerful monarch by whom the land that had afforded him shelter was ruled."— Rundall's "*Memorials of Japan,*" Preface, p. iv.

commend themselves by their truth alone; they then examined what had been done by men in international transactions, from the earliest times on record, though they did not accept or approve everything that had been done as a precedent, but adopted as precedents and examples, to be followed only by such acts or modes of transacting international business as agreed with the eternal principles of truth and justice, which they took as the point of departure for ascertaining what international law was, or should be: they also related various wrongful transactions, as examples to be avoided.

In the nineteenth century "Civilisation" has taken the place of "Religion" as a watchword, and as a pretext for aggression. The modern term, like the former one of difference of religion, is used to proscribe those who differ from the persons who utter it, and to deprive them of those rights which all men possess in common, and to get rid of those obligations which all members of the family of mankind owe to one another. The modern term is more vague, more elastic, more unjust; and it serves to deprive the Chinese of the rights of international law and its mutual obligations, equally with the Feejee Islanders, or other cannibals.* The application of the

* The following passage from a controversy between Las Casas, bishop of Chiapa, and Dr. Gines de Sepulveda, chronicler of the

word "Civilisation" is very much like that of "Orthodoxy;" it claims pre-eminence for the speaker who uses it. The possession of civilisation cannot alter right or wrong, remove obligations, or lessen the necessity of observing good faith with the uncivilised, any more than a difference of religion can do any of these things. Yet people now-a-days reason, and certainly governments act, as if this were the case. On the contrary, the claim to a higher civilisation, so far from freeing those who make it from their obligations to those whom they term uncivilised, imposes upon them the duty and the neces-

---

Emperor, at Valladolid, in 1550, lays down the obligations of civilised nations towards cannibals, and those whom they consider as such. The former says :—

"The fourth argument of Dr. Sepulveda is founded on the injury which the Indians inflict upon the innocent; killing them to sacrifice or eat them. To which the Rev. Bishop, although in the sixth case he had conceded that it was incumbent upon the Church to defend the innocent, answered that it was not, however, a convenient or suitable thing to defend them by wars. This he based upon three or four grounds. The first has already been touched upon, that of two evils we ought to choose the lesser; and that the Indians should kill a few innocent people to eat them, which is even more revolting than sacrificing them, is without comparison a lesser evil than those which come of war, from the excesses of which many more innocent persons are killed than the number of innocent persons whom it is proposed to liberate. In addition to this, by these wars the faith is brought into ill repute and made odious to the unbelievers, which is even a still greater evil. The second argument was because we have a nega-

sity of making good their claim, by superior respect to what is lawful, just, and true.

Since civilisation confers no rights over the uncivilised, it is not strictly necessary to inquire what is civilisation, or by what it is tested. M. de Maistre limited it to those nations which study Latin. M. Escayrac de Lauture claims civilisation for all those countries which possess fire-arms and the printing-press. Mr. Cobden would assign the highest civilisation to the country possessing the greatest number of miles of electric telegraph and the largest quantity of daily newspapers. The Chinese might point to

---

tive precept, 'Thou shalt not kill;' and most particularly, '*insontem et innocentem non occides*,' (Exod. xxiii.), which is more rigid than the affirmative one to defend the innocent. And on this account, when it is not possible to accomplish this second precept without going against the first, the second ought rather to be broken than the first. And since in the fights of nations in a just war, where there are cities of the enemy, several innocent people may be killed accidentally, not knowing them, and without any such intention; yet when war is undertaken to chastise some delinquents, if it is to be presumed that the innocent persons are in greater number, and that it is not possible to distinguish between the two, it is a sounder counsel to omit to inflict such chastisement, conformably with the evangelical precept of Jesus Christ, who did not permit the plucking out of the tares from the wheat, lest instead the wheat should be plucked out at the same time, but He rather chose that it should be deferred till the harvest, which is the day of judgment, when it will be possible without risk to discern the good and the bad, and to chastise these without prejudice to the others."

respect for the law, and the most ancient annals; and the Japanese might put forward absence of pauperism as tests of civilisation, worth at least as much as the others: they could, at any rate, maintain that civilisations differ like religions, but that there is no foundation for the claim of Europeans to be the sole possessors of the former.

The use of unmeaning terms has superseded the sense of law; and that superiority of civilisation should have been put forward as a justification for international acts, which would not have been tolerated, or even attempted between European nations, shows how much the study of international law has been neglected of late, and how much its first principles have been set aside and contemned. The confusion arising from this contempt of international law, begun in Asia, is now spreading to Europe; and the evil must increase, unless some great writer should arise, with power to recall and enforce upon the present generation the forgotten lessons and the high morality of Grotius, and the other writers who followed him.

Meantime, it may be well to reiterate some of the principles laid down by those great men; especially those, the neglect and transgression of which have led to disorders and wars, to the demoralisation of states, and, subsequently, of individuals.

One of the first principles of international law is, that all nations are equal, without regard to their size or importance, or to the form of their government; since the duties of nations towards each other are the same as those of individual men towards their fellow-men, and a dwarf is as much a man as a giant.* It follows from this, that nations are bound to assist in the preservation of other nations; to assist them in cases of famine and calamity; to contribute towards their improvement, but not by forcible means, or against their will; to cultivate the friendship of other nations; to take care of their honour; and the differences of religion should not prevent one nation from rendering to another services of humanity, and no nation should do anything to injure another; and the intercourse between nations should be mutually beneficial. Yet what is the practice, and, apart from positive aggressions, how is it that public morality in England has sanctioned the enforced introduction of opium into China, in spite of the laws of the country, and whilst opium is an unmitigated evil, a means of debauchery, admitting of no palliation?

It is equally well established, that no nation has the right to interfere in the internal affairs of

* Vattel, "Preliminaries," book ii. chap. i. sect. 18.

another.* Yet of late it has been assumed that two or three nations could, by joining together, acquire a right against a third which they did not possess separately. This practice has been protested against under the name of Non-intervention, and this has been made a principle and a virtue. But we do not talk of non-robbery or non-piracy, so that this term shows the demoralisation of opinion; for it leads to the supposition that intervention or non-intervention are different policies, instead of the true notion that intervention is wrong and cannot, in any manner, be justified. Wheaton, after referring to the refusal of England to join in the measures of interference taken by the Congress of Verona, in 1822, seeks to justify the intervention of France, England, and Russia, in 1827, in the affairs of the Morea.† It was open to any of those countries to have sent an ultimatum and a declaration of war to the Ottoman Porte, but the conduct which led to Navarino, and warlike operations in the midst of peace, was a distinct violation of law, and a crime.‡

Partly owing to this setting aside of the principle of equality amongst nations, by fanciful divisions of civilised and uncivilised; partly owing to interven-

* Vattel, book ii. chap. i. sect. 7.
† Wheaton, vol. i. part ii. chap. i. sect. 9.
‡ The case of Mexico is so recent that it is enough to name it.

tions, by which hostile acts are committed against nations with whom those who intervene are not at war, great abuses, irregularities, and violations of the law have taken place in the manner of carrying on war. To make war lawful or just, it is necessary that one nation should have a cause of complaint against the other; it is necessary that a remedy should first be sought for the injury complained of, that, if redress is refused, an ultimatum, threatening war, should be sent to the state causing the injury; and lastly, that war should be formally declared, and the causes of it proclaimed, by the sovereign of the state which complains of the injury. Such is the law of nations.* The law of England is the same; and it requires that a declaration of war shall have been made by the sovereign, without which no acts of war are lawful, and they are in nowise distinguished from piracy.†

Vattel's words upon the necessity of a declara-

---

* Vattel, book ii. chap. xviii. ss. 334, 354, 378; Grotius, book iii.

† This has been proved by a decision in the case of Evans *v.* Hutton, in 1842, given by the Chief-Justice Tindal, and the judges Coltman, Erskine, and Maule. This case was an action for breach of contract. The defendant had contracted to land the plaintiff's goods at Canton during the year 1839, but was prevented from doing so by Captain Elliot, the Superintendent of Trade, and Captain Smith, of Her Majesty's ship Volage. The decision was for the plaintiff. The judges unanimously held, that no orders

tion of war, and of avoiding its calamities if possible, should be ever present to those who think so lightly of undertaking military operations. He says:—

"The right of making war only belongs to nations as a remedy against injustice: it is the fruit of an unfortunate necessity. This remedy is so terrible in its effects, so fatal to humanity, so vexatious even to him that makes use of it, that national law doubtless permits it only at the last extremity; that is, when every other is of no avail for upholding justice. It has been proved in the preceding chapter, that in order to be authorised to take up arms it must be, 1stly, that we have a just subject of complaint; 2dly, that we have been refused a reasonable satisfaction; 3dly, we have also observed that the ruler of a nation must take into mature consideration whether it is for the good of the state to pursue its rights by force of arms. This is still not enough, as it is possible that the imminent fear of our arms may make an impression upon the mind of our adversary, and oblige him to render us justice. We owe yet this concession to humanity, and, above all, to the blood and repose of the subjects, to declare to this unjust nation, or to its ruler, that we are going to have recourse to the last remedy, and to employ open force to bring it to reason. This is what is called *to declare war*.

---

in council having been alleged, the proper authority which Captain Elliot possessed among British subjects in China, as Superintendent of Trade, had not been made out. They further held, that *no declaration of war* having been alleged, it could not be pretended that what he did was in exercise of *the Queen's undoubted prerogative.—Report of the East India Committee of the Colonial Society, on the Causes and Consequences of the Military Operations in China,* p. 39. London, 1857.

All this is comprehended in the manner of proceeding of the Romans . . . It is surprising to find amongst the Romans conduct so just, so moderate, and so wise, at a time when it would seem that nothing but valour and ferocity was to be expected of them. A people which treated war in so religious a manner, established very solid foundations for its future greatness."*

Vattel then states, that the declaration of war should recite the subject of complaint for which arms have been taken up; and explains that war should not be carried on if, after it has been declared, the enemy should offer equitable conditions of peace.†

Let us inquire into a few recent instances of warlike operations, and see how far they were undertaken in contempt of these canons of international law.

In the Afghan war there was neither declaration of war nor just cause of it, since the motive assigned was the desire to meet and anticipate Russian influence. The China war was undertaken without a declaration, or a just cause of war, since it arose from the attempt to enforce the introduction of opium, a prohibited article, into China. This and the Afghan war have been so much written about, that it is sufficient here to allude to them.

In 1858 an infuriated crowd attacked the British

---

* Vattel, book iii. chap. iv. sect. 51.
† Ibid. book iii. chap. iv. sect. 54. Grotius, liv. ii. chap. xxiv. sect. 1; liv. iii. chap. iii.

Consul at Jiddah, and killed him, and then proceeded to murder the French Consul and some Greeks who were in the town. As soon as the news was received, the Sultan sent assurances to the British and French Embassies that the matter should be inquired into, and the guilty punished: his Imperial Majesty, at the same time, sent a sum of money from his privy purse to be distributed amongst the relatives of the victims. Here, so far from there being any disposition to refuse redress for an injury, the state in which the injury was done anticipated any demand for it, so that no cause of war could arise. If the state injured was not satisfied with the redress offered, it was open to it to withdraw its ambassador, and declare war. Notwithstanding this, the British Government, at the same time that it was receiving assurances of redress, sent telegraphic orders to Captain Pullen, of H. M. ship Cyclops, to bombard Jiddah, which orders he executed. This precipitation is entirely contrary to the deliberation which should precede war, according to all writers on international law: an act of war without a declaration of war was committed, and that whilst negotiation was going on. The guilty in Jiddah deserved punishment, but it was for their sovereign to punish them, and a foreign state had no right except to call upon him to do justice. Such an event could not have occurred, but for the utter disregard and disrepute into which international law has fallen.*

The same disregard for law, and preference of might to right, was shown in the bombardment of Kagosima. Satisfaction for the death of Mr. Richardson had already been given by the Japanese Government, in the shape of an indemnity of one hundred thousand pounds; and by asking for, and accepting that indemnity, the British Government had precluded itself from further action.

In 1852 a French fleet appeared before Tripoli, in the west, and made a demand, the justice of which was doubtful. On the demand being refused, the French, instead of treating the matter at Constantinople, threatened to bombard the town; and the Governor was compelled to yield to save it from bombardment.

The evils of these departures from law and usage multiply themselves and increase. Cabinets issue instructions to carry out acts of war without a previous declaration of war in the name of the Sovereign, and now subordinate governors improve upon this practice, and carry on military operations without even the sanction of instructions from home. Recently, in 1862, the Governor of Singapore sent

* For the misconduct which provoked the massacre see the two preceding essays.— *Editor.*

to the Sultan of Tringganu, who is entirely independent of the British Government, to demand the expulsion from his city of the Sultan of Lingga, nephew of the ruler of Tringganu. The ground for this demand was the allegation that the Sultan of Lingga abetted disturbances in the neighbouring state of Pahang—also an independent state. But as the Sultan of Tringganu is tributary to Siam, the Governor of Singapore also wrote to Bangkok, to complain of the presence of the Sultan of Lingga at Tringganu, and to ask for his removal. The Governor of Singapore did not, however, wait for an answer to this application to Bangkok, but sent a peremptory demand, backed by a naval force, to Tringganu, for the expulsion of the Sultan of Lingga. As the ruler of Tringganu had no orders to receive from the Governor of Singapore, he naturally refused to violate the duties of hospitality by compliance with this ultimatum; the consequence of which was, that the naval force sent from Singapore bombarded Tringganu. This act of war, besides being unlawful and unjust, was gratuitous and useless; for, almost at the same time that the bombardment was going on, the Siamese answer to the Governor's application was being sent to Singapore, to the effect that the Siamese Government would send a steamer to Tringganu and recall the Sultan of Lingga. The

Siamese Government naturally protested against this unlawful and unnecessary violence; but, apparently, without any beneficial result. The conduct of the Governor of Singapore was disapproved of,* but in terms such as leave it to be supposed, that whilst the injudiciousness of his policy was apparent, its violation of international law had passed unperceived; and the door was not closed, as it should have been, upon the possible future commission of similar unlawful acts.

After this came the Ashanti war, the existence of which was only known to the nation after its fruitlessness and disastrous consequences had become public. Here, again, no declaration of war had been made; and in this instance the value of such a declaration, as concerning the interests of the nation commencing war, as laid down by Vattel, became apparent: for if the facts which became public in the course of the debate in the House of Commons had been known at the outset, it is probable that the same result, of refusing to sanction these hostile operations, would have been arrived at without the loss of life and expenditure which occurred. If it is objected that the formalities of a declaration of war were superfluous with the Ashanti kingdom, it may

* Parliamentary papers relative to bombardment of Tringganu, 1864.

be answered that international law makes no distinction with regard to states: that law and right are to be observed, for the sake of fulfilling a duty by the person that observes them, on their own account, and irrespective of other considerations. And, lastly, as it appears we had an extradition treaty with Ashanti, if the kingdom of Ashanti was thought worthy of international stipulations, other international usages should have been complied with.

Besides, disregard of right in dealings with one country serves as an example for a similar disregard in another; the evil extends and increases, till the habitual mixing up of war and peace in China has confused the public mind to such an extent that public approbation was given to the expedition of Garibaldi to Sicily, which in no respects differed from the attempt of the Savoyards to seize upon Geneva, in 1602, by escalade. The Savoyards failed in their attempt, and all their prisoners were hanged. Vattel quotes this as an instance of brigandage rather than of war,[*] and says of the execution of the prisoners, that "Geneva was not blamed for an action which would have been detested in a formal war."

In explaining that no nation has a right to meddle with the government of another, and that no sove-

---

[*] Vattel, book iii. chap. iv. sect. 68.

reign can set himself up as a judge of the conduct of another, Vattel* blames the conduct of the Spaniards who brought the Inca Athahualpa to trial: he says, "If this prince had violated the law of nations with respect to them, they would have had the right to punish him. But they accused him of having put to death some of his subjects, of having had several wives, &c.—things of which he had no account to give them. And what crowns their extravagant injustice, they condemned him by the laws of Spain." Two similar instances of violation of international law have recently occurred, which it is well to mention as examples to be avoided. When the Siamese conquered Keddah, assisted by some British gunboats, which blockaded that port, one of them commanded by Captain Sherard Osborne, the Sultan of Keddah was driven out, but continued to wage war upon the Siamese. For this he was subsequently brought to trial in a British court of law in the Straits Settlements, on a charge of piracy: the decision was an acquittal, on the ground that he had not been engaged in piracy, but in lawful war. But the court had no right of jurisdiction, and the prosecution should not have been entertained. Its institution was a continuation of the injustice which had been done to the Sultan of Keddah by the Straits

* Vattel, book ii. chap. iv. sect. 55.

Government in blockading Keddah and assisting the Siamese, whilst the stipulations of the treaty with Keddah, under which England holds Pulo Penang and Province Wellesley, especially provide that England should *defend* Keddah from any enemy coming by sea.*

The motive for this action of the British Government, so much in opposition to the treaty engagements, was the desire to obtain a commercial treaty with Siam: this policy, nevertheless, entirely failed in its object, and a commercial treaty was not negotiated with Siam till many years later. Still more recently a similar abuse of jurisdiction took place at Singapore. An action was brought into court there against the ruler of Johore, for acts of his in Johore complained of by a Chinaman. Judgment was given against the ruler of Johore: this decision was, however, reversed at Calcutta, where it was ruled that the court had no jurisdiction in the matter.

A most flagrant violation of international rights was committed in the summer of 1864, by the French Consul at Tunis, who "warned off," and attempted to prevent the landing of, the Ottoman

---

* An additional illegality was perpetrated against this ruler of Keddah, for after this trial and acquittal, instead of being released, Tunku Mahomed Said was detained a prisoner for many years; which imprisonment was wholly illegal.

Commissioner; that is, an officer of the sovereign of the country. The relations of France with Tunis (those of a neighbour) would not have justified the French Consul with interfering with a public officer deputed by any other state, much less then with an officer sent by the sovereign. It was said at the time that the French Government disapproved his conduct, but the disapproval was not, as it should have been, public as the offence. The consequence of this act remaining unpunished and unnoticed, has been a repetition of the offence a few months later in an aggravated form, as narrated in the following letter given in the "Times," as received by its Malta correspondent from an authentic source in Tunis, and dated Nov. 17:—

"A singular incident has just occurred here. From time immemorial it has been customary for the Sultans to send Commissioners to Tunis, and for the Beys to depute Envoys to Constantinople, either to compliment the Sultans on their accession to the throne, or to solicit their own firman of investiture, or on other matters connected with the affairs of the two countries. At the breaking out of the revolt, the Sultan despatched an Imperial Commissioner to Tunis to report on the state of affairs; and, in return, the Bey had formed a resolution of sending an Envoy to thank his Imperial Majesty for the interest he had evinced in passing events. According to custom, he announced his intention to the foreign representatives, in order to obtain from them letters of introduction for his Envoy to the Ambassadors at Constantinople; but the French Consul, upon being made aware of the Bey's intention, proceeded immediately to his Highness, and remonstrated in the strongest possible terms against an envoy being sent to the Sultan without the previous sanction of the French Government. He insisted that it was an Anglo-Turkish intrigue, which he would not tolerate. In vain did the Bey endeavour to explain that it was customary both to receive and to send envoys; and that, in the present instance, it was an act of courtesy towards the Sultan, who was the head of all Mussulman nations; and that nothing more was either meant or intended. The Consul would accept no explanation; said that the Envoy could not leave without his permission, but that he would despatch an *aviso* to Cagliari with a telegram to Paris; and that until he received a reply the departure of the Envoy must be postponed. His Highness having, however, replied to his peremptory language, that he was at liberty to send for instructions, but that he did not intend to alter his resolution of showing respect to the Sultan, by deputing General Khaireddin to convey to him his grateful thanks; the French Consul rose, evinced much impatience, and left the room, after crying out 'No! no! no!' when he refused to take the hand which the Bey had offered to him. This unfortunate incident, coupled with a previous threat of sinking the Sultan's Commissioner, when he arrived in May last, in case he should attempt to land, determined the Bey, with a view to avoid further embarrassment, to hasten the departure of his Envoy, who was therefore directed to proceed on his journey on the 14th, instead of the 17th inst. General Khaireddin, consequently, embarked on board the Tunisian steamer Bechir, about half-past six in the evening; but a French officer was sent to him on the part of the commandant of the ironclad, Invincible, stationed at the Goletta, to dissuade him from proceeding on his journey; and when he was told that he was bound to execute his orders, the officer announced to him that, in that case, he would be prevented. General Khaireddin then said that he should follow instructions, and would only yield to superior force, as he was not authorised to lose the steamer and sacrifice the lives of the crew. He gave the officer sufficient time to carry his answer to the captain of the Invincible, which was all this time firing rockets and burning blue lights, when he weighed anchor, and at half-steam passed the ironclad. When about 1000 yards ahead of her, the Invincible chased the Tunisian steamer, which put on full steam, and kept ahead of her pursuer, until they both neared the Island of Zembri, at the entrance of the bay, when the Tunisian steamer boldly passed through the Straits between the island and the mainland. It being perilous for a large vessel to attempt the passage at night, the Invincible had no other alternative but either to make the circuit of the island or return to her anchorage. She preferred the latter course, and the Tunisian steamer and Envoy thus escaped being captured in Tunisian waters by the vessel of a foreign and a friendly power. This affair, which is attributed to the political intemperance of the French representative, has created a very painful sensation in Tunis. It has utterly disgusted the Tunisian authorities; and it has humbled the Europeans to think that so open a violation of every principle of public right and international law should be perpetrated by the agent of a great and powerful nation against a weak government, which it pretends to protect against the encroachments of others."*

Another fruit of the aggression on China has been a similar aggression on Cochin-China. France had no just cause of war in Cochin-China, for if any of her Missionaries were killed in that country the fault was theirs, and their going there and preaching in defiance of the Government was in

* This Consul has been removed in consequence.

itself an aggression.* France, however, did not carry war into Cochin-China only for the sake of avenging a few Missionaries; they may have been the pretext: but the motive was to seize upon the country for the sake of establishing a colonial empire, and following the example of England. England, however, was more to blame than for her example only; for had she not invited the co-operation of France in China, and so occasioned the despatch of twelve thousand troops to China, it is doubtful if France would have sanctioned the sending of those troops to Cochin-China only for the problematic establishment of a colony: but the French nation imagined, when these troops were sent to China, that they were sent for our assistance, and in return for concessions to be made by us in their Italian policy, and much bitterness was felt and expressed by them when they found these hopes disappointed. A treaty has just been concluded by France with Cochin-China, restoring part of the conquered territory and retaining a "protectorate" over another part, with an indemnity of a hundred millions of francs to be paid to France.† It was not to be expected that the example set in

---

* Vattel, book ii. chap. i. sect. 7.

† This treaty has not been ratified, and France retains the conquered provinces.

China should not be followed, especially since bad examples are more readily followed than good ones. When neighbouring nations quarrelled and fought there usually was some excuse, if not in the amount of injury of which one or other had to complain, at least in the mutual animosity and strife fomented by long years of rivalry; but in the case of these distant nations beyond the seas, those excuses are wanting: feelings of hostility do not exist, and these wars, so lightly undertaken, have a strong similarity to brigandage. They have another base feature, in that they are all waged by the powerful against the weak, and so can boast of none of those acts of valour and daring which give a relief to wars amongst equals, and which ennoble the career of the soldier fighting for his country in a just cause. For the justice of the war not only adds to the fame of the soldier, but it augments his valour. Grotius insists much upon this point, and condemns mercenaries,* and soldiers who, fighting for pay or plunder, make a trade of war. It is on this point that Vattel falls below Grotius, for, being a Swiss, and seeing what the Swiss practice was, he accepted in this respect what existed, without examining whether it was right, and he attempts to defend

---

* Grotius, liv. iii. chap. xxv. sect. 9.

mercenaries on grounds of utility and advantage.* That Grotius is right and Vattel wrong is proved by the fact, that whilst formerly soldiers trading in wars just or unjust, in the service of foreign princes, were called, and called themselves, ."mercenaries," this name has now become a term of reproach, and such troops are now designated as "foreign legions." On this point the opinion of an eminent author may be cited:—

"It is one very awful form of the operation of wealth in Europe, that it is entirely capitalists' wealth which supports unjust wars. Just wars do not need so much money to support them; for most of the men who wage such, wage them gratis: but for an unjust war, men's bodies and souls have both to be bought; and the best tools of war for them besides, which makes such war costly to the maximum . . . And all unjust war being supportable, if not by pillage of the enemy, only by loans from capitalists, these loans are repaid by subsequent taxation of the people, who appear to have no will in the matter; the capitalists' will being the primary root of the war: but its real root is the covetousness of the whole nation, rendering it incapable of faith, frankness, or justice, and bringing about therefore, in due time, his own separate loss and punishment to each person."†

To conclude, there is no mystery in international law; and though every one may not study it, each man may understand what are international

* Vattel, book iii. chap. ii. sect. 13.
† Ruskin's Essays, "Unto this Last," p. 154. London, 1862.

rights and duties, by becoming convinced of that which forms the basis of international right; and that consists in the consideration of nations as individuals, and in the fact that there is no separate standard between states and individuals: for as individuals compose a nation, so nations compose humanity; and the rights of nations and their obligations to each other in no wise differ from those which exist between individuals; and as the law, whether criminal, civil, or poor law, recognises no difference between men of different classes or religions, learned or unlearned, in the same manner international law, which depends upon right and wrong, which are immutable, cannot vary between nations, however different their position in the world may be. And the key-stone of international as of individual duty is the Divine command, to "do unto others as you would they should do unto you."*

* "What is permitted to one nation is permitted to every other, and what is forbidden to one nation is equally forbidden to every other."—*Vattel*, "*Preliminaries*," sect. 19.

"The seat of judicial authority is indeed locally here in the belligerent country, according to the known law and practice of nations, but the law itself has no locality. It is the duty of the person who sits here to determine the question exactly as he would determine it sitting at Stockholm; to assert no pretension on the part of Great Britain which he would not allow to Sweden in the same circumstances, and to impose no duties on Sweden as a neutral country, which he would not admit to belong to Great Britain in the same character."—*Lord Stowell.*

All the false notions which now obtain with regard to international obligations have come in under cover of the phrase, "Religion has nothing to do with politics."

By means of this phrase, such words as policy, expediency, and other ambiguous terms, invented to cover a dubious transaction, have led men to approve of in public matters what they would condemn in private matters. Religion means a sense of accountability in a future state, and so religion has to do with every act that men can do in this world; and if an account has to be given for every idle word, surely public acts affecting a large number of fellow-creatures must be still more a subject of account than private acts affecting the happiness only of a few.

IV.

ISLAM AS A POLITICAL SYSTEM.

(WRITTEN IN 1833.)

"Never in the course of their history have Mahometans been brought into contact with any form of Christianity that was not too degenerate in its rites, its doctrines, and its effects, to be worthy of their esteem."—*Smith and Dwight's "Missionary Researches,"* vol. ii. p. 334.

DURING that distracted period which followed the Greek war, I happened to be present at the sack of a Greek village by Albanians. After the seizure or destruction of the little it contained they turned their eyes to a chapel which stood at some distance, and made a rush in that direction, either with the view of securing, or of destroying and insulting, the remnants of its service and the symbols of its worship. As they reached its threshold a Mussulman Dervish suddenly presented himself, and grasping with extended arms both posts of the door exclaimed, "You can only enter here over my body." At the time I believed the contest to be religious and right on the side of the Christians, because of the fanaticism of the Turks. Words cannot render my astonishment: I saw that I was wholly in error, and I applied myself to inquire. It is with a profound consciousness of incapacity that I approach this subject. It is to a future age that it will remain to analyse that portion of the history of man, our general ignorance of which is summed up in the word " Mahometanism."

Islam is divided into two portions—Imân (Faith), and Dîn, which I will render, Practice. It comes nearer to the French term *culte*. It is not the dogmatic, but the practical portion of Islam which has influenced the moral, social, legal, and political ideas and circumstances of its professors. This, then, is the branch to which I will apply myself. The hold it has over man we naturally refer to its dogmas, because such is the only hold that religion has over us. Our religion is neither the rule of the courts of law, nor does it decide upon the policy of the state. We, therefore, hold religion and policy different things, and do not, even in expression, so much as conceive a connexion between religion and jurisprudence. What, then, are to us religion, institutions, and honour—powerful as motives, but distinct in their application, and sometimes opposed —is for them all contained in that one word,

"Islam." It is patriotism, legality, tradition, constitution, right.

While I separate dogma from practice, referring the constitution of Eastern society to the latter, still the dogma has materially affected this state of the East, in consequence of the influence of Christian feelings on the policy of Eastern Governments. However contrary such impulses may be to that charity which is the essential character of true Christianity, and to those interests which it is the avowed purpose of that policy to sustain, I am, therefore, induced to say something on this head, convinced that the Christian who knows their belief will cease to revile; and when he observes the influence of their devotional feelings on their lives, will deem them worthy of sympathy, if not of imitation.*

The unity and the immateriality of the Deity is the grand doctrine. The contemplation of the greatness, power, and goodness of God, is the devotional exercise. The five cardinal points are,— the Profession of the Faith; Prayer, called by Mahomet the pillar of religion and the key of

* I once heard an American Missionary at Constantinople, distinguished for his zealous and successful efforts (Dr. Goodall), thus address some young Missionaries who were expressing themselves contemptuously of the Turks,—" You will see practised here the virtues we talk of in Christendom."

Paradise; the Fast of Ramazan; Almsgiving, which is a practical regulation of the charity inculcated towards their fellow-men. The Pilgrimage to Mecca was but a regulation, in accordance with previous habits, to maintain the unity of doctrine, and to refresh the zeal and ardour of its professors. The injunction regarding washing and cleanliness is an accessory to prayer. Sale, in his " Preliminary Dissertation," p. 139, says :—

" That his followers might be more punctual in this duty, Mohammed is said to have declared that the practice of religion is founded on cleanliness, which is the one half of the faith, and the key of prayer, without which it will not be heard by God. That these expressions may be the better understood, Al Ghazali reckons four degrees of purification; of which the first is the cleansing of the body from all pollution, filth, and excrement; the second, the cleansing of the members of the body from all wickedness and unjust actions; the third, the cleansing of the heart from all blameable inclinations and odious vices; and the fourth, the purging a man's secret thoughts from all affections which may divert their attendance on God; adding, that the body is but the outward shell with respect to the heart, which is as the kernel. And for this reason he highly complains of those who are superstitiously solicitous in exterior purifications, avoiding those persons as unclean who are not so scrupulously nice as themselves, and at the same time have their minds lying waste and overrun with pride, ignorance, and hypocrisy. Whence it plainly appears, with how little foundation the Mahometans have been charged by some writers with teaching or imagining that these formal washings alone cleanse them from their sins."

The Mussulmans believe with the Christians in an Omnipotent God, Creator of all things; in the immortality of the soul; in the resurrection of the body; in the recompense and punishments of a future life. In respect to the remission of sins and justification, the Mussulman comes much nearer to the Calvinist than some other sects of Christianity (and they compose by far the greatest portion) who admit of works as justification. They believe with the Unitarians, Socinians, Arminians, and other sects, in the prophetic character of Christ.* They believe with the Lutherans, Calvinists, &c., in justification by faith, and not by works, and with the latter sect in predestination. While subordinate to those distinctions they concur with Protestantism in the grounds of its separation from the Church of Rome.

* "I have, I think, put the parallel between Mahometanism and Socinianism in a pretty clear light. I could carry it farther to the disadvantage of our Unitarians, who are at a greater distance from the truth than the Mussulmans in the articles of the creation, of the knowledge of God, of providence, of predestination, and of the state of human souls after death."—*Catholic Tract*, quoted by *Mr. Forster*, vol. ii. p. 500.

"Jesus Christ is revered by all the doctors as the greatest of the Prophets before the Arabian Legislator; as the Messiah of nations and the Spirit of God. The Saviour is regarded as predestined to return in the plenitude of ages, to reassemble all men in unity of one belief."—*D'Ohsson*, vol. i. p. 427.

"The Christian heretics all verge towards Unitarianism, that is, Mahometanism."—*Mahometanism Unveiled*, vol. i. p. 305.

Very possibly I may surprise the reader when I state that the Mussulmans believe in the inspired writings, at least in the Pentateuch, the Psalms of David, and the Gospels. A Mussulman may differ from a Christian in the interpretation of a passage, but he does not deny the " Law and the Testimony." The sects of Christianity with which the Mussulmans have come into contact can scarcely be said to have had the Bible.

The character of Mahomet is, perhaps, the point which has produced the most unfavourable impression on Christians. But, in fact, we have erred in this matter. He himself disclaims the power of working miracles, does not pretend to salvation out of good works, nor is he designated by his followers by any other title save that which is common to Abraham, Isaac, and Jacob, and which is used to one another at the present day by friends in familiar discourse. Anything more would be inconsistent with their all-absorbing idea of the Deity. Mahomet is not ranked so high by the Mussulmans as are the saints in the Romish Church. But a large portion of the Mussulmans, the Wahabees, had rejected even the use of that name by which we chose to know the body. In the formula of their faith they have substituted, in the place of *La illahá il'Alláh Muhammad resul Illah* (There is no Deity but God, and Mahomet is the apostle of God), *La illahá il' Allah malik yaum eddin* (There is no Deity but God, the Lord of the day of judgment). Now the doctrines of the Wahabees were admitted by so many of the Ulemah, in every portion of the Empire, to be in strict conformity with the original principles of their faith, that the suppression of that sect was felt to be the only means by which a political division of the Ottoman Empire could be prevented; and the Western Mussulmans lent themselves to the purposes of the state on this occasion, through the apprehension of the consequence of the hostility of Christendom in the event of any division taking place between the Mussulmans. The Wahabee reformation would have brought Islam into the closest resemblance with Protestantism; and it is curious to remark, that while the use made of the prejudices of Christians has prevented this consummation, millions of Christians* have apostatised through the violence of a European power, who has acquired this means of indirectly propagating Islam from the support it obtains from Christian fanaticism.

At the time of the Reformation, the Mussulmans

---

* The Circassians, the Lesghis, &c. See "Progress of Russia in the East," by Sir John M'Neill.

were considered as religious allies.* To say nothing of Lollards and other sectarians, fellowship with them was admitted by Cromwell, and unambiguously expressed by Queen Elizabeth, in a letter to Sultan Murad. If, as Iconoclasts, the Catholics conceive that they ought religiously to be made war upon, and expelled from Europe, it might have been imagined that the Protestants, in parity of reasoning, would have taken the opposite view of the question.† The fact is, that the intercourse of latter times between the East and the West has consisted in a reverberation of prejudice and an exchange of wrong.

The following extracts from the orthodox creed will not be read without interest:—

" Praise be to God, the Creator and Restorer of all things, Who does whatsoever He pleases, Who is Master of the glorious throne and mighty force, and directs His sincere servants into the right way and the straight path; Who favoureth

---

* There are, in Count Mailette's "History of Hungary," some curious facts respecting the mutual good will of the Turks and the Protestants, which the author had difficulty in reconciling with the received notions, and therefore represented the Turks as disposed to abandon Islam, because, where they had no mosques, they frequented Protestant churches.

† "The Mussulmans are Christians, if Locke reasons justly, because they firmly believe the immaculate conception, divine character, and miracles of the Messiah."—*Sir William Jones*, "*Asiat. Resear.*" vol. i. p. 275.

them after their having borne testimony to the Unity, with the preservation of their confessions from the darknesses of doubt and hesitation ;* Who directs them to follow His chosen Apostle, upon whom be the blessing and the peace of God! Who maketh known to them, as touching His essence, He is One and hath no partner; Singular, and hath no like; Unique, having no contrary; Separate, having no equal. That He is Ancient, having no first; Eternal, having no beginning; Everlasting, having no end; to be described by glorious attributes; subject to no decree; determined by no limits or times; but is the First and the Last, and is within and without.

"Neither doth He exist in anything; neither doth anything exist in Him; neither is there anything besides Himself in His essence; nor is His essence in any other beside Him. And that as to the attributes of His perfection, He wants no additional perfection. And He is known to exist by the apprehension of the understanding, and is seen, as by ocular intuition, out of His mercy and grace, by the holy in the eternal Mansion, completing their joy by the vision of His glorious presence.

"And that He (praised be His name!) is living, powerful, mighty, omnipotent; not liable to any defect, or impotence; Who neither slumbers nor sleeps, nor is obnoxious to decay nor death. To Whom belongs the kingdom, and the power, and the might. His is the dominion and the excellency, and the creation and the command thereof; the Heavens are folded up in His right hand, and all the creatures are couched within His grasp. His Excellency consists in His creating and producing; and His Unity in communicating existence, and

---

* The difference between the Sheeites and the Soonees is one, according to our ideas, of a political rather than of a religious character. It is, indeed, considered religious by themselves, because with them everything is religion.

Original. He created men and their works, and measured out their maintenance and their determined times. Nothing can escape His grasp that is possible; nor the vicissitudes of things get out of the reach of His power. The effects of His power are innumerable, and the objects of His knowledge infinite.

"Now He produced creatures anew for the manifestation of His power and His precedent will, and the confirmation of His word, which was true from all eternity; not that He stood in need of them, or wanted them: and that He manifestly declared His glory in creating, and producing, and commanding, without being under any obligation; not out of necessity, since loving-kindness, and showing favour, and grace, and beneficence belong to Him; whereas it is in His power to pour forth upon men variety of torments, and afflict them with various kinds of sorrows and diseases; which, if He should do, it would be justice in Him; not reproachful, nor injustice. And that He rewards those that worship Him for their obedience upon the account of His promise and beneficence, not of their merit, nor of necessity; since there is nothing which He can be tied to perform, nor can any injustice be feigned in Him, nor can He be under any obligation to any person whatsoever.

"*But that the creatures are obliged to serve Him ariseth from His having declared, by the tongues of the Prophets, that it was due to Him from them; not by the simple dictates of the understanding, but that He sent them Messengers, whose veracity He had proved by manifest miracles,*[*] *who brought down from Him to men commands, and promises, and threats.*

"Furthermore, that He doth speak, command, forbid, promise, and threaten by *an eternal ancient Word, subsisting in*

---

[*] This does not refer to Mohammed, who disclaimed the power of working miracles.

His essence. . . . And that the Koran, the Pentateuch, the Psalms of David, and the Gospels, are books sent down by Him to His Apostles."

The foregoing will suffice to show that their belief warrants the conclusion to which I have been led by experience, that the Mussulmans entertain no antipathy to the Christians on religious grounds. I shall now address myself to the civil and political branches of the system.

Islam is regarded in Europe as a "religion of blood," and as having extended itself by the sword. Whatever, or however favourable may be the opinions of any person in reference to Oriental manners and Turkish character, this anti-social maxim is held to be a fundamental portion of their belief and their institutions. If it be erroneous, great is the wrong we do, and how universal!

The small beginnings of the system render it difficult, if not impossible, to conceive how it could progress by physical means, and through the violation of law and policy. Here no numerous race adopted suddenly a principle of intolerance; here no antiquated system became inquisitorial and fanatic, and used the authority acquired, and the power realised, by the virtues of ancestors, to trample on the outraged feelings of man or the laws of nature. Islam, so wonderfully successful as a system as to reach almost to its full growth in its earlier infancy, could only progress through superiority over coeval systems.*

Mahomet was the only founder of a religion who was at the same time a temporal prince and a warrior. Their power lay exclusively in restraining violence and ambition; his temptation was ambition, and the sword was at his disposal. It is therefore to be expected, that making religion a means to temporal power, and having obtained that sway over the minds of his followers, by which they accepted as law and right whatever he chose to promulgate, his code should be found at variance with all others, and even in opposition to those dictates of justice which are implanted in the breasts of

---

* One of the courtiers of Heraclius thus explained, in a council at Antioch, the cause of the astonishing and alarming progress of the Arabs:—

"The victories of the Arabs are to be ascribed solely to the perfection of those institutions and of that religion by which they were restrained from evil and stimulated to the performance of virtue. From this alone, and from no other circumstance, they derived those irresistible energies which, as men and as soldiers, gave them a decided superiority over all that had been employed against them."— *Price's* "*Mahometanism,*" vol. i. p. 71.

After several chapters, in which the Arabs are only mentioned as fanatics, spreading their creed by the sword, Major Price slips in the following observation:—" It may be once for all observed, that in the early stage of their progress towards foreign dominion the disciples of Mahommed were *seldom, if ever,* known to be *extremely urgent* for a change in point of faith."— P. 93.

all men. If, then, we find that it is not so—if we find him establishing maxims of right in international dealings, of clemency in the use of victory, moderation in that of power, above all, of toleration in religion, we must acknowledge that, amongst men who have run a distinguished course, he possesses peculiar claims to the admiration of his fellow-creatures. The Arabs were a people of rapine. His followers implicitly believed, and this was all his world. There were no nations around whose feelings he had to respect, admiration to win, or censure to dread: his conduct is therefore referable solely to his own internal instincts, and to that obedience to the whisper of conscience which must be a condition of all greatness, and in which may truly be said to reside the character of man; the germ of which, though born with each of us, has on this populous earth, during the ages of its existence, so seldom ripened to maturity.

A private man made himself to be looked upon as a prophet by his own family. A simple Arab united the distracted, "the scanty, naked, and hungry tribes of Arabia," into one compact and obedient body, and presented them with new attributes and a new character among the people of the earth. In less than thirty years this system defeated the Emperor of Constantinople, overthrew the Kings of

Persia, subdued Syria, Mesopotamia, Egypt, and extended its conquests from the Atlantic to the Caspian and the Oxus; from which limits, during twelve centuries, its political sway has never receded, while the faith has continued to extend, and is at this hour extending in Northern Asia, in Central Africa, on the Caspian, and the Adriatic.

A combination so extraordinary, and events of such magnitude, flowing from the ideas patiently developed during fifteen years by a solitary Arab, friendless, unknown, and dwelling in the desert or the cave, are not to be explained by phrases, whether employed by the vulgar or the philosopher. These changes were not effected by the outpouring of nomade hordes, by the progress of military aggression, or the gradual extension of diplomatic dominion; they were brought about within a single lifetime by men's thoughts, and have endured through forty generations, not through prescription, but by attachment.

Islam has never interfered with the dogmas of any faith, never persecuted, never established an Inquisition, never aimed at proselytism. It offered its religion, but never enforced it; and the acceptance of that religion conferred co-equal *rights* with the conquering body, and emancipated the vanquished states from the conditions which every conqueror, since the world existed up to the period of Mahomet, has invariably imposed. For its proselytes there was no obligation of denial and revilement of their former creed; the repetition of a single phrase was the only form required or pledge exacted.*

The two great faiths with which it stood in opposition, Judaism and the Greek Church, were declared to be the models, and their "Book," or Bible, the fountain of the faith of Islam; at the same time it swept away the power and taxes usurped by the Church, which at that period oppressed the Christians of the East not less than the political despotism under which they groaned, while it also diminished a very large proportion of the religious observances, penances, and superstitions previously in force in both religions; preserving in this respect a happy medium between the conservation of prejudices deeply rooted and the destruction of practices associated with them which had become too onerous to bear.

It is not at the present day that we can judge of the effect of a conqueror preaching to his subjects and a general praying with his men. It is not at

* Gibbon says, "The repetition of a phrase and the loss of a foreskin," was all that Islam required: but circumcision is not obligatory.

the present day that we can estimate the awe and respect imposed upon mankind, the enthusiasm and devotion animating the people, or the phalanx who proclaimed the majesty of God, and the necessity of His worship through the observance of good faith between man and man; who exhibited examples of love in the household, devotion in the temple, union in the camp, valour in the field: who associated with themselves at once the loftiest conceptions of natural devotion and the most trivial observances of personal cleanliness.

The faiths with which it stood in competition were Christianity, chiefly as represented by the Greek Church; Judaism, then possessed of great political and military power; and Fire-worship. With the latter we have little to do, although it is also associated with Islam in reference to all the doctrines which it holds in common with Christianity; as, for instance, that most remarkable of all, the resurrection of the body, re-promulgated on the banks of the Oxus 600 years before the Christian era. As regards Judaism and Christianity, Islam adopted them as its models; they were the sources of its faith. The same revered personages were alike prophets and teachers for all three; there was blood alliance.

Islam did not rise under any persecution from these creeds. There could be no bitterness, even of circumstances. In Arabia its first persecution was by, as its subsequent wars were carried on with, the local idolatry, and in the course of this period the Jews and the Christians in Arabia seem to have been considered its allies: it was impossible that there could be rancour against either, and unless such a passion had existed in the highest degree, it was impossible to make religion the ground of a war of invasion. These considerations appear to me to supersede all argument, and to put aside all testimony; the thing was impossible.

How the reverse should be stated by the Mussulman and Christian writers of early times, and, consequently, thereafter believed, is easily explained. To the Mussulman the word Religion stands in lieu of State. Where we would say, "There was a meeting of the people," they would say, "There was a meeting of believers." Every act is referred to God; all authority thence derived. War was with them a judicial matter, so that they would speak of religion commanding a war as we would speak of religion commanding charity, or love, yet without the one being more an act of fanaticism than the other. This is a general habit of mind and form of expression, but there then comes a purposed misapplication, to prove its claims to Divine favour. The Mussulman would speak of his religion as being propagated by the sword;* which words, indeed, would strictly signify that his side had triumphed. The Christian writers in the same spirit would assert the same thing, as charging violence and injustice on their antagonists. Besides, to Christians a difference of religion was, indeed, a ground of war, and that not merely in dark times and by fanatics. The great restorer of international law in Europe, Grotius himself, formally excepts the Mussulmans from all participation in the community of rights which he lays down, and the permanent piracy of Malta was sustained by the chivalry of Europe, and into it were periodically drafted the scions of its noble, princely, and regal houses. I may further add, that throughout the Mussulman world the belief that the sword is the weapon of Christianity is quite as common as in Christendom that counter-belief which we are examining.

The expansion of Islam is, therefore, to be looked for in its own inherent character, in the genius of its

---

* Amongst them the sword does not represent the idea of violence; and so the succession of the Caliphate was by Mahomet remitted to the sword. It conveyed the sense of an appeal to the God of Battles—a judicial duel.

founder, in the qualifications of its earliest apostles, the system of its political administration, the condition of rival creeds, and the circumstances of surrounding nations: and if it be a rule of philosophy to content ourselves with sufficient causes for any effect, and to abstain from introducing hypothetical ones, we will be dispensed in this case from admitting the argument of religious compulsion, which would not only be superfluous as an hypothetical cause, but destructive of the practical ones which account for the result.

At the time that the Mussulmans crossed Arabia Petræa, and showed themselves in Syria, the two great empires of the East, the Greek and the Persian, and the two religions which prevailed in these states, were alike corrupt and tottering, oppressive to the nations by hopeless burdens and intolerable observances; revolt and schism were the common characters of both, and the appearance on their respective thrones of princes of extraordinary spirit and capacity had only the effect of adding hatred, invasion and war, to the sum of the calamities of each, severally incapable of reconstruction. The Christians in their internal schisms sought support from the Parsee Monarch, and on the metaphysical points of Unitarianism and Dualism, as bearing on the nature of Christ. The warlike inhabitants of the mountain ranges, extending from the Euxine down to the borders of Egypt, having taken the side opposed to that then espoused by Heraclius, these countries, on religious grounds, were more favourably disposed to the Persian than to the Christian monarch. Religious animosity being thus fervidly excited at home, was in abeyance as between Christian and Parsee. The power of the two states was equally in abeyance. The history of time will therefore not afford a conjuncture more favourable for the interposition between them of a new system, at once religious and political, respectfully observing the creed of each, and employing the sanction of its new faith to establish beneficial maxims of civil and political freedom. These were the two conditions of respect for religious feelings, subversion of governing system, so as to induce the people to make a sacrifice in regard to the first in order to secure the benefits of the latter. This is precisely what was done. The Unitarian doctrine of Islam, in the sense of the Godhead, fell in with the Unitarian doctrines of the Monophysites and Monothelites, with respect to Christ; indeed, the same terms were used for both; and that hitherto unobserved coincidence of Islam with the Mazdasnians might seduce the Persians into the belief that they had but modified the forms of their Church without abandoning its profession.* Islam put an end to infanticide, then prevalent in the surrounding countries. Christianity might be equally opposed, but was not equally successful. It put an end to slavery, the adscription to the soil.† It gave equality of political rights, and administered even-handed justice,‡ not only to those who professed its religion, but to those who were conquered by its arms. It reduced taxation; the sole tribute to the state consisting of the tenth. It freed commerce from all charges and impediments; it freed the pro-. fessors of other faiths of all forced contribution to their Church or their clergy, and of all religious contribution whatever to the dominant creed. It communicated all the privileges of the conquering

---

* I can do no more than here indicate the importance of the language then employed with reference to the terms. Throughout the mountains, from the Taurus downwards, the Syriac was then in use. The Armenians had adopted the Chaldaic and Syriac characters and religious literature, so that their religious shibboleths consisted, as against the Greek and the doctrines of Constantinople, in those very identical terms by which Islam appears in the present day to place itself in opposition to Christianity.

† Slavery in the East is not the slavery of Europe, as this single incident will show. Othman, to appease the tumult in which he perished, offered freedom to the slaves who would *lay down* their arms.

‡ In reporting a case between an Arab and one of the princes of the tribe, the Caliph Omar says,—" I told him (the Prince) that that was no matter, for they were both Mussulmans, and therefore equal."

class to those of the conquered who conformed to its religion, and all the protection of citizenship to those who did not. It secured property, abolished usury, and the private revenge of blood.* It inculcated cleanliness and sobriety: it did not inculcate them only, but it produced and established them. It put an end to licentiousness, and associated with charity to the poor the forms of respect for all. Success in either of those points was enough for the triumph of any system.

Such were the offensive weapons of Islam. Conversions with these wings flew so rapidly in the rear of the Black Eagle of the Saracens, that future

---

* On the occasion of the last pilgrimage that the Prophet of the Arabs conducted to Mecca, he is represented "pronouncing as he went along a discourse of singular sublimity and eloquence, in which he solemnly declared the property of his followers, as well as their persons, reciprocally sacred and inviolable to one another, *in the same degree as they held the solemnities in which they were mutually engaged that day, in the same sacred place.*" "Know," said he, "that I have brought under foot the institutes and usages of ignorance and infidelity. The homicide, therefore, which previously occurred among you, I also absolve from revenge; and the blood for which I shall first pronounce absolution is that of my cousin Rebbiah, the son of Mareth. In the same manner, and with the same solemnity, have I abolished the usurious practices of the period of reprobation; and the contracts of usury which I shall first prescribe and annul are those of my uncle Abbas, the son of Abdul Mutaleb, in order that revenge for blood and claims for usury may be first abrogated in my own family."—*Price's* "*Mahometanism,*" vol. i. p. 608.

ages, seeing nothing but victories, have accounted for the inexplicable fact by an impossible theory.*

Instead of Islam having introduced a bloodthirsty spirit amongst the Arabs, it had precisely the contrary effect. Mahomet, from reasons which the event justified, refused to appoint his successor, notwithstanding his own anxious desire that a certain man should succeed him. He did everything to induce the people to select Ali, though he would not nominate him. He went even so far as to place him on the Minbar above himself. Ali, though invariably regarded as the first of the Mussulmans, was passed over on three elections. It was not that he was judged to be deficient in any of the qualities requisite for a chief, but because he was a man inured to bloodshed. Speaking of the election of Abu Beker, Major Price says,—"But this was only the first of three successors in which the pretensions of the distinguished chieftain Ali were baffled or overlooked, with no other exception to his choice than that (*among a nation of homicides*) he was alleged to be a man of blood. Not less decisive are the epithets of those preferred to him—Abu Beker, the *just;* Omar, the *patriarchal;* Othman, the *pacific.*"

* "On *one* day, no less than 20,000 Christians, Jews, and Magians, embraced the Mahometan faith."—*Sale,* "*Preliminary Discourse,*" p. 209.

M

Having thus shown, on general grounds, the unlikelihood of the existence at the basis of this system of so anti-social a principle, I must now proceed to the proof of my proposition, which is to be found in their law; and I assert that in that volume, which by common consent is held to contain, not merely the maxim but the injunction of propagating religion by the sword, there is not one line at variance with the common instincts of humanity, or with the law of nations, as laid down by our first writers, however disregarded in our present practice. I might content myself with this declaration, and throw upon my antagonists the burden of disproof; I might ask them to produce their counter-authorities, and as they can produce not one, the case is closed. But I will go further. I will disprove them out of their own mouths. I select their highest authority, Sale. He says:—

"Under the head of Civil Laws may be comprehended the injunction of warring against Infidels, which is repeated in several passages of the Koran, and declared to be of high merit in the sight of God: those who are slain, fighting *in defence* of the faith, being reckoned martyrs, and promised immediate admission to Paradise."

Will it be believed that there is not a single passage in the Koran to justify this assertion? He refers, in a foot-note, to a variety of texts: there is not one of those texts which does not controvert him, as will be seen presently when I cite them from his own translation. He was misled by the expression, "Fight for religion," which is constantly used, and which, as I have above shown, implies the same as with us would be implied by the words, "Fight for your rights," "Fight for your country."* Sale being considered a partisan of the Mussulmans, his opinion has been considered conclusive; and who would venture to question a maxim for which a score of references are given to the Koran itself? and these words of Mahomet, applied to his small band of persecuted followers, to encourage them to resist attack, are received to-day as a command laid on 150,000,000 of men to assail all other creeds. Now, here are the passages referred to in the note:—

"And fight for the religion of God against *those who fight against you; but transgress not by attacking them first:* for God loveth not the transgressors."—*Koran*, chap. ii.

"If they (the true believers) ask assistance of you on account of religion, it belongeth unto you to give them assistance; except against a people between whom and yourselves there shall be a league subsisting; and God seeth that which ye do."—Chap. viii.

"God hath purchased of the true believers their souls and their substance; promising them the enjoyment of Paradise, on condition that they fight for the cause of God. Whether they slay or be slain, the promise is assuredly due by the Law (of Moses), the Gospel, and the Koran."—Chap. ix.

But who are the unbelievers? those "who have

* See note at the end of the Essay.

violated their oaths." . . . "Will ye not fight against those who have violated their oaths, and have conspired to expel the Apostle of God, and who of their own accord assaulted you?" Sale adds the following note:—" As indeed the Koreish, in assisting the tribe of Beer against those of Kozaah, had laid a design to ruin Mahomet without any just provocation."*

" If God did not repel the violence of some men by others, verily monasteries, and churches, and synagogues, and the temples of the Moslems, wherein the name of God is frequently commemorated, would be entirely demolished." Sale's note to this passage is:—

" This was the first passage of the Koran which allowed Mahomet and his followers to *defend themselves against their enemies by force*, and was revealed a little before the flight to Medina; till which time the Prophet had exhorted his Moslems to suffer the injuries offered them with patience: which is also commanded in above seventy different places of the Koran." †

I need not multiply instances.

What a contrast have we not here with the then practice of the world, and even with its maxims! At the period of Mahomet's rise, a state of public law, if the term can be so used, had been superinduced by the connexion of the schisms of the

* Chap. ix. † Chap. xxii.

Eastern Church with state policy, whether as regards internal revolution or conflict with Persia, similar to that which arose out of the Reformation, when a difference of religion became, on the one side, the basis of an alliance, and on the other, grounds of war. Amongst us the rectification took place through the labours of jurisconsults, in which the Jesuit Suarez and the Reformer Grotius took the lead; and gradually Europe was brought back to see that rights were not contingent upon faith. It was the founder of a new religion, himself chief of the state and leader of its armies, who, in the seventh century, proclaimed this truth, and specially asserted it for the benefit of the professors of other faiths. Islam may, therefore, be said to owe its extension to its assertion of international law.

As to the systems from which Mahomet copied, of course he found in Christianity the purest and most benevolent of maxims; but he was liable to interpret the Gospel by the acts of its followers, or would have been so, had he not been gifted with that intuitive perception of the means of influencing mankind which involves all practically important truths. The same thing may be said in reference to the religion of Jemshid, known by the name of its reformer, Zoroaster; for the majesty of its ancient principles had likewise been obscured. The third system, however, Judaism, did give a religious sanction to aggression; not with a view of conversion, but of extirpation. The Jews were cursed for sparing. Mahomet quotes both Moses and David to justify war, but applies the example to defensive ones.

But we must look at conduct as well as maxims.* Perchance in this case, as in many others, the one may belie the other. The first wars of Mahomet in Arabia were defensive. The war with the Greek Empire arose out of the assassination of an envoy. The career once entered upon, they were placed in just warfare with the whole of the then world. It was impossible that aggressive war should not take place; but I confine myself to the original code, and the early period by which its character was formed and its principles fixed. The spirit of aggression never breathed itself into that code which formally incorporated the law of nations as a portion of the faith, and the Mussulmans, in the hour of triumph, were always ready to say, "Accept our faith, and you will cease to be even tributary; you will enter into full fellowship with the conquering people." It is this, which was a generosity then undreamt of, which became the ground of the charge in practice of propagating religion by the sword. As these

---

* See note at the end of the Essay.

charges rest principally upon the events of the first and great war — that of Syria, I cannot avoid referring to them, as given by Alwakidi, vehemently disposed to make every war a religious one, and every victory a sign from Heaven. Here is the instruction of the Caliph on the first foreign expedition :—

"When you make any covenant or article stand to it, and be as good as your word. As you go on, you will find some religious persons that live retired in monasteries, who propose to themselves to serve God in that way."

The following is the account of the capture of Tyre :—" Youkinna, the governor of Aleppo, had turned Mussulman, and had introduced himself into Tyre with 900 followers, also converts to Islam. His design and character being discovered, he and his men, on the approach of a Saracen force, against whom the governor had sallied forth, were confined in the Castle. A Christian named Basil, holding some place of trust in the Castle, released these men while the two armies were engaged without the walls."

"This Basil, upon information of the great success of the followers of the Prophet, was abundantly convinced of the truth of his mission. This inclined him, having so fair an opportunity offered, to release Youkinna and his men, who, sending word to the ships, the rest of their forces landed and joined them. In the mean time, a messenger in disguise was sent to acquaint Yezid (the Saracen leader) with what was done. As soon as he returned, Youkinna was for falling upon the townsmen upon the wall; but Basil said, perhaps God might lead some of them into the right way, and persuaded him rather to place the men so that their coming down from the wall might be prevented. This done, they cried out, '*La illahê!*' &c. The people perceiving themselves betrayed, and the prisoners at liberty, were in the utmost confusion; none of them being able to stir a step, or lift up a hand. Those in the camp hearing a noise in the city, knew what was the occasion of it, and Youkinna opened the gates and let them in. Those that were in the city fled, some one way and some another, and were pursued by the Saracens and put to the sword. Those upon the wall cried quarter. Yezid told them, that since the city was taken by force they were all slaves. 'However,' said he, 'we, of our own accord, *set you free, upon condition you pay tribute; and if any of you has a mind to change his religion he shall fare as well as we do.*' The greatest part of them turned Mahometans."

" When Constantine heard of the loss of Tripoli and Tyre his heart failed him; and, taking shipping with his family and wealth, he departed for Constantinople. All this while Amrou Ebn ul Aâs lay before Cæsarea. In the morning, when the people came to inquire after Constantine, and could hear no tidings of him nor his family, they advised together, and with one consent surrendered the city to Amrou; paying down for their security 2000 pieces of silver, and delivering into his hands whatsoever belonged to Constantine that he had not carried away with him. Thus was Cæsarea lost in the 17th year of the Hejrah, and the fifth of Omar's reign; upon which those other places in Syria which as yet held out, namely, Ramlah, Accah, Joppa, Ascalon, Gaza, Sichem (or Nabolos), and Tiberias, surrendered; and in a little time after the people of Beirout, Sidon, Jabalah, and Laodicea, followed their example: so that there remained nothing more to be done in Syria, but all was entirely subdued by the Saracens, who had not spent above six years in subduing that large, wealthy, and populous country."*

From Syria the arms of the Arabs were turned against Persia, and the deputies of Omar offered to Yesdegird terms by which war might be avoided— the profession of Islam and *the reform of political abuses;* all taxes to be reduced, save the tenths, and 2½ per cent of every man's means for the poor, the distribution of which was left to himself; justice to be administered by the code of Mahomet; and all men, without distinction of grade or office, to be subject to it. Such terms did no more agree with the dispositions of Yesdegird than with those of any other monarch; and he, his nobles, and the chiefs of the priesthood, were cut off in the desperate stand they made amidst millions of indifferent subjects.†

The communication made by the Saracen General to the Governor of Egypt is also equally decisive :—

"Abadah (the emissary of Amr) coming into Makouka's presence, he bade him sit down, and asked him what they (meaning the Arabs) meant, and what they would have. Abadah gave them the same answer as the Saracens always used to do, to all that asked them that question; telling him that he had three things to propose to him by the command of Amr, who had received the same order from his master, Omar the Caliph, viz. that they should either change their

---

* Ockley's "History of the Saracens."
† Price's "Retrospect of Mahometanism," vol i. p. 105.

religion and become Mahometans, and so have a right and title to all privileges in common with them, or else pay perpetual tribute yearly, and so come under their protection; or else they must fight it out, till the sword decided the controversy (not of faith, but dominion) between them."

On this Ockley remarks:—" These, as we have observed before, were the conditions which they proposed to all the people where they came; the propagating their religion being to them a just occasion of making war upon any nation whatsoever."

The propagating their religion could not have been the occasion of their making war, as it was not the object of the war, nor the consequence of triumph. Ockley's supposition would be incorrect, even if they had proposed conversion or tribute, for they were already at war with the empire to which Egypt belonged.

A spirit the very reverse of this is evinced in every page of the history of Islam, in every country to which it has extended; so that in Palestine a Christian poet* has exclaimed, twelve centuries after the events to which we are referring,—" The Mahometans are the only tolerant people on the face of the earth;" and an English traveller† reproaches them with being too tolerant.

The results produced by Islam seem too vast, too

---

* Lamartine. † Slade.

profound, too permanent, to allow us to believe that the human mind could anticipate them, far less adjust the scheme; thence the disposition to take refuge in chance, or providential design, instead of applying to it the process of reasoning, by which we estimate the effects of the laws of Solon, or the triumphs of Timoleon. Nevertheless, this scheme was framed by a single man, who filled with his own spirit those who were in immediate contact with him, and impressed a whole people with the profoundest veneration of which man ever was the object. The system of laws and morals which he formed agreed equally with the highest development as with the lowest level of society, which, during ten centuries, passing from race to race, made every people by whom it was received superior to, and triumphant over, the nations and empires with which they came in contact.

By the same process that Islam subdued Arabian idolatry, so did it subdue fire-worship. After conquering the Arabs it conquered the Persian Turks, Mongol Tartars, Berebers, and a large portion of the Greek and other populations. At this day that faith is spread where the hostile banners of its professors never flew. Missionary labours have extended it to the eastern confines of India. Moorcroft found it in Ladak, triumphing over Buddhism; and the Landers found it on the banks of the Niger, putting an end to human sacrifice, where its sway is established with regal pomp and despotic power. No one ever heard of inquisition into man's faith, or conversion by force; and where the title of High Priest and Successor of Mahomet is placed above that of emperor and of king, no follower of a different creed contributes from his substance to the maintenance of the Church. Whilst Turkey was an aggressive power, it might have been politic in the nations she attacked to raise the cry of religion, but as against an unaggressive state it is as insane as it is immoral. The present fomentation of revolt amongst its Christian subjects is undertaken out of the same regard for the propagation of Christianity as the fomentation of internal discord, or the military survey of the frontiers of India for the propagation of Islam—for the dupes in the one case are the victims in the other.

To the mind of the Mussulman, no idea of antithesis is conveyed by the designation of his faith with that of Moses or of Christ. He holds these to be stages of progression, and thence the expression, "A Jew must become a Christian before he can be a Mussulman." He calls Abraham and the Patriarchs Mussulmans. He says all men are born Mussulmans. Islam means "resignation." They do not call us Christians, but followers of Hazret Isa, the blessed Jesus; the reviling of whom is blasphemy, and is punished with death.

In the time of Mahomed IV., a Christian priest had made profession of Islam, and, to prove his zeal, reviled our Saviour, applying to him the epithet "impostor," which he had been accustomed to apply to Mahomet. The Mussulmans, shocked at the outrage, carried him before the Divan, and he was ordered for immediate execution.*

This chapter having been translated to a party of Mussulman doctors at Constantinople, one of them inquired, at its conclusion, why I had taken so much trouble to write down these things. I explained what were the prevailing ideas in Europe. He then retorted, "In that case you have not said half enough," and said that I should refer to every war which had occurred during the last 150 years, every one of which had arisen out of the religious animosity of Christians. "When," said he, "has Turkey violated a treaty, or undertaken a war, save in self-defence? And what, on the other hand, has

---

* "Mahomet was the wilful prey of his own unbridled passions; Christ, the perfect pattern of all virtue. The only comparison open to us is one of contrast, and the only appropriate contrast, that between 'the swine wallowing in the mire and the Lamb without blemish and without spot.'"—*Forster*, vol. ii. p. 479.

This from a "Christian philosopher;" what might be expected from an illiterate monk?

been the conduct pursued towards us? The violation of every moral and religious feeling; not only treaties violated, and aggressive and unjust wars undertaken, but treaties falsely interpreted, and the agents of all powers, and even our own, turned against us. Then, our subjects, urged to insurrection on the grounds of religion, and ourselves attacked by the three greatest powers of Europe, in profound peace. Now you accuse us of being the aggressors, and attribute to our religion the hostility of yours. After the battle of Navarino, what was it that saved your lives and your property but our respect for the precepts of our religion? Ask the Greek inhabitants of Arnout-Keuy to whom they owed their salvation from inevitable destruction?" I inquired, What were the circumstances to which he alluded? He told me, that on the breaking out of the Greek revolution some thousand Asiatic troops were embarked at Constantinople, to be sent to Galatz, but the wind proving unfavourable, the vessels cast anchor in the Bosphorus, at that village. Infuriated against the Greeks, these troops determined on burning the village, which was exclusively inhabited by Greeks. They were on the point of carrying their design into execution, when the Greeks sent information of it to one of the body of the Ulema, who resided in the neighbourhood.

He immediately assembled as many of the Ulema as were within reach, and as no time was to be lost, they hastened to the beach, carrying with them all the money they could collect. "What," said my informant, "were the arguments they used? Were they not the words of the Prophet? and why did they venture themselves on so perilous a service, but because they were his servants and the guardians of the honour of the Mussulmans?"* "But," said he, "so strongly impressed on every true Mussulman is the obligation of having right on his side before he has recourse to arms, that if the Russian fleet were to sail down the Bosphorus not a gun would be fired until the signal for hostilities was given by the invaders themselves. Ask the Russians if they have not, at the commencement of every war, taken cruel advantage of this conscientiousness on our part, even when dealing with men who have never used to us the words 'faith' or 'honour' but for purposes of fraud and deceit?"

The foregoing pages were returned to me by a friend, to whom I had submitted them, with this remark,—"This is all very well, and I will take your word for it, but this is only one half of the question; let me now see the defects of Mahometanism; for like the moon, its emblem, it must have its dark side."

---

* This fact has been confirmed to me by the inhabitants of Arnout-Keuy.

I confess I was startled with the observation, because I had only been struck with the good parts, and had only thought of these. I had at the time to deliver myself from a most inveterate censure, an implacable hatred; and consequently, as I gradually came to admit what was good, I dropped my own previous opinions as to the bad: and in fact, in all inquiries, it is the good alone that links on, connects thought, or strikes root. In this case, moreover, it was the branch of the subject which presented novelty. But, desirous to yield to my friend's wishes, I looked up the subject in travellers' and other books, and made a catalogue of the evils of Islam. I found to my surprise, that there was not one of these which I could not show to be a misprision, or a calumny. Of course it will be understood that I am speaking of it as a political system, and considering it simply as a code of laws. I set down face to face the allegations, with my remarks:—

1. IMPOSTURE IN RELIGION.   With this I have nothing to do.

2. SENSUAL PARADISE.   This is also a religious point; but it is to be observed that the descriptions of the Koran are spiritually explained and understood, as is by us the Song of Solomon.

3. No Souls allowed to Women. — An ignorant mistake.*

4. Sensuality. — They bring that charge against us. Napoleon observes that Mahomet was the only Eastern legislator who *restricted* the number of legitimate wives. I refer the reader on this head to the chapter entitled "The Life of the Harem," in "The Spirit of the East."

5. Religious Schism. — The schisms of Islam are not doctrinal; not even that between the Sunnys and the Shiahs.† It is remarked by Sylvester de Sacy, in his "History of the Druses," that the early spirit of Mahometanism was devotional, but not doctrinal. The metaphysical spirit was a subsequent importation from the Greeks and Persians.

6. Extension of Religion by the Sword. — A mistake.

7. Persecution of other Creeds. — Ditto.

8. Intolerance. — The reverse of the truth.

---

* See note at the end of the Essay. † Ibid.

9. Enmity to Science and Letters.

Islam has outstripped the enlightenment of our age by making instruction a fundamental law.* Every child must be put to school in its fifth year. It is the duty of the state to instruct the citizen, that he may understand the laws he has to obey, and of the family to teach the child the means by which he may acquire his livelihood. Every Sultan is instructed in a handicraft, and some of them have earned thereby their subsistence. There have been, however, no educational heart-burnings, because each community had to teach its children for and by itself. It was from the Mussulmans that Europe received science and letters.

10. Burning of the Library of

This event, however it may have occurred,† was followed

---

* At Constantinople, when a quarter is burned down, the inhabitants are obliged to rebuild the school, but the mosque is not rebuilt until provided for by its own endowments, or by some pious person.— *Note of Editor.*

† It is most doubtful that this event ever did occur, since it is not related by contemporary Arab historians, and the wilful burning

ALEXANDRIA.

seventy years after by the reign of Mostassem Billah; and if the event is a charge, that reign might be a redemption. Speaking of it with Mustafa Pasha, of Skodra, he said, " It was a crime of self-defence; the faith was young." The present Mussulmans, indeed, say, all science is to be found in the Koran, but they did not burn Ulug Beg. The present scientific darkness of the East has as much to do with Islam as that of the eleventh century in the West with Christianity.

11. PUNISHING OF APOSTATES WITH DEATH.

I am not going to defend this law, but I nevertheless enumerate it in the list of unjust charges, for it is one which Christians have no right to make, and which, in a practical point of view, is utterly insignificant. If we are con-

---

of a library would have been contrary to the precept of Mahomed,—" Seek for science, even though it be in China;" and the saying of Abu Hanifah,—" Thank the Greeks for paper, for which you are indebted to them." However, the burning of all the Arab works on history, medicine, and agriculture, by Cardinal Ximenes, on the ground that they were Alkorans, is historical.—*Note of Editor.*

11. Punishing of Apostates with Death.

trasting two systems of long duration, to judge of their character from their conduct, we must not take the opinions of a certain period of the one as the test by which we shall rate the whole course of the other. Let us go back three centuries, when rival fires were being lighted by Christians to burn the bodies of other Christians, and who would have dreamt of bringing this law as a charge against Islam? I have already said that religion includes country, consequently this law is the law of treason. As to its abolition having any effect in influencing religious opinion, I utterly deny it. If there was a disposition towards conversion, it would be thereby increased, and almost without exception; the instances, rare as they are, of its application, have been those of Christians who first apostatised and then relapsed. However, this law, by what I must call a most cowardly, as well as ill-judged, violence on the part of

11. Punishing of Apostates with Death.

the British Embassy, has been now, so to say, superseded. We will see whether conversions will be the result. Any one acquainted with the people will be of a very different opinion. It opens the door to apostasy, because it withdraws that which has been hitherto the great obstacle, the impossibility of returning thereafter to their original faith. Death is very different for a Mussulman and for a Christian. Besides, the tide of conversion is running the other way. No one has ever heard of a Mussulman becoming a Christian, but millions of Christians throughout the Ottoman Empire have, in the course of the last century and a-half, become Mussulmans.

12. Separation of the Sexes.

This, like the former, is indefensible in itself. That women should veil up their faces, and be separated in society from men, no natural law commands, and no necessity will justify; but if we estimate an institution by its effects,

12. Separation of the Sexes.

that is to say, if we compare its effects with those of other institutions, I do not think that we shall have grounds for condemning this one. I believe that in the East domestic happiness is realised in a greater degree than in Europe: at all events, there is no compulsion. The people like their way of life, and compulsion would be required to alter it. This, however, like the former point, was not a new law introduced by Mahomet, but an institution existing from the earliest times.

13. Slavery.

Again a mistake, resulting from the false application of our own terms. When an anti-slavery despatch was sent to Lord Ponsonby, he refused to communicate it to the Turkish Government, and in his reply asked with what face he could deplore the miserable condition of the slave to a Reis Effendi or a Grand Vizier, who was himself a slave.

14. Immutabi-

This is an opinion, and not a

LITY OF LAW ARRESTING PROGRESS.

charge. There are those, even amongst ourselves, who side with the Mussulmans. The value of this objection, says Richardson, regarding the Institutes of Menu, depends upon the character of the law, and it is clear that laws that are not good cannot be immutable. It is clearly as desirable to keep good laws as to change bad ones, and so in fact we may both be right. In any system where the laws are immutable there must be simplicity in the machinery, and facility of the adaptation to practice; as, on the other hand, where the principle of change is admitted, the best of laws must lose half their value. It will scarcely be denied that amongst us legislation is but the tool of party, and the expression of the despotism of a temporary majority with the effect of complication and multiplicity, which imply badness of law.

15. VENALITY OF JUDGES.

Throughout the history of Islam this has been the great

15. Venality of Judges. cause of commotion and the butt of satire; yet, perhaps in no country is less injury suffered from legal proceedings. There are no lawyers; proceedings are immediately brought to a close. Judicial authority is, moreover, recognised in all municipal and elective officers; all corporations, religious communities and commercial guilds, administer justice through their own officers, without interference from the tribunal; their civil awards are enforced by their own authority; their penal decision (death excepted) by the Turkish authorities.

16. Despotism. Turkey is the only government in the world which is not struggling with its people to wrench from them their privileges. It is, on the contrary, engaged in an attempt to confer them. A Sultan can impose no tax, make no law, declare no war, contract no debt. If the constitution of Islam were translated and applied to any country in Europe, it would be

CHARGES BROUGHT AGAINST IT.

16. DESPOTISM.

17. ABUSES OF ADMINISTRATION.

considered a beautiful, but impracticable, theory of Utopian freedom.

This, it will be observed, is a practical, and not a theoretic point.* The Turks established themselves by conquest, which exposes a people and a system to temptations which almost inevitably end by its ruin. Two questions then arise: first, whether the abuses have their root in the system? the second, whether they be capable of remedy? I answer negatively to the first, and affirmatively to the second; and I but repeat the opinion, and, at that time, the prophecy of the first authority on the subject, D'Ohsson,† who at the very darkest period of Turkish history asserted that those abuses were capable of easy rectification, because not in the system, and because they were violations of positive canon law.

---

* See note at the end of the Essay.

† "Tous les maux politiques qui affligent les peuples Musulmans dérivent de leurs préjugés, de leurs fausses opinions, des vices du gouvernement, mais non des vrais principes de la religion et de la loi."— *Mouradyia D'Ohsson.*

18. FATALISM. I know not how to answer a charge conveyed by a word which has no meaning. They do not believe in Fate, and cannot, therefore, believe in an abstraction of Fate. They do assert man's free-will; they hold him responsible for his acts before God and man; they do not believe only, but trust in Providence. Their dispositions differ from ours in many respects, but not as the result of vain speculation. They are content when they have no grounds for being dissatisfied, and are, consequently, inert where Europeans would be busy. They are resigned to the decrees of Providence, and, consequently, quiet where the European would be dissatisfied. They do not believe in the contagion of the plague, and, consequently, attend the sick-bed of a relative when a European would be touching him with a pair of tongs, or flying into the country. And they are in the habit of saying on all oc-

18. FATALISM.   casions "God is great," and so leaving the morrow to take care of itself. A Turk could not deny that he was a fatalist, for the best of reasons—that he has no such extravagance in his brain, or such a term in his language.

Such is the catalogue of evils, as I find them in European writers. I may be considered partial in this statement, yet no one has the experience of the evils of Turkey that I have had, because my work in that country has consisted in a struggle for their rectification. My support in this has been always the Koran, and in so far as I have succeeded, it has been from this cause. If I have spoken commendatorily of them, it is not to themselves. With them, the theme has ever been their wrongful judgments and abusive acts; but so conscious are they of their own departure in this respect from the original type, that instead of being looked on, in consequence, as an enemy of Islam, my crusade, if I may so call it, has gained me the designation of "Threefold Mussulman." However, other Europeans have come to the same conclusion. I have already stated that of D'Ohsson; I will add that of a powerful French writer who had every opportunity of knowing them,—

"Islam is neither the enemy of progress nor the friend of violence and abuse."

This search after faults has led me to the observation of two points, in which Islam is superior to all other systems. The decrepitude of all beliefs is the putting the creature in the place of the Creator. Islam is old enough to have experienced this change; yet alone has it remained free from idolatry and superstition. In regard to the second point, the contrast is rather with Christianity than with Buddhism or Brahminism; it has reference to international law; it deals with the acts of the community, as our courts of justice with the acts of the individual. No doubt the Christian religion, and more specifically the Old Testament, forbids alike crime in the community and crime in the individual; but Christianity established no court for the enforcement of that law; and having gradually emerged from a condition of obscurity and persecution, there was never formed a system of administration which, so to say, should apply and implement the faith. It is true that the Church exerted itself to control, through the consciences of men, the lawlessness of princes and the passions of people; and we find it interposing, denouncing, and excommunicating, with the effect of diminishing the frequency, mitigating the savageness, and limiting the duration of wars, and thus establishing a rule and code of right and honour, out of which came the chivalry of the middle ages, which is of scholastic and monastic parentage. But in all this the Church was an *opposition*, not an institution—a petitioner for justice rather than the judge dispensing it from the bench. The feebleness of this organisation is exhibited at later times, when the Church was reformed; when, instead of supplying the fundamental deficiency, or strengthening the power it still retained, the Reformation purposely ruptured the connexion between the Church and the aggregate conscience, saying to it, " You shall be spiritual only; you shall be little children, and yet preach to grown-up men ; but all that regards justice and judgment, that is, 'policy,' is no matter of yours." In the end it has happened, that the nations of Christendom have lost and entirely forgotten, to the very tradition, the meaning of *war*, beyond the mere material facts connected with it ; so that the perpetration of a national murder, entailing the loss of tens or hundreds of thousands of lives on the parts of those whom we assail, or in retribution for our own act, can be effected without so much as the formalities requisite for cutting a road or building a bridge. Justice in its highest sense has disappeared from Christendom; with it, Religion, in its social and binding power; and it would require a very fine distinction—so very fine that I am unable to perceive it—to admit of the possibility of the existence of faith, in the abstract sense, amongst a people on whom judicial blindness has fallen. A man who has committed a murder may be a Christian, but no one will say that that man is a Christian who is ready daily to commit murder. There is no difference in regard to morality between a collective and an individual murder; and if a community continues to remain aware, in its private dealings, of the distinction between murder and self-defence, while it has lost that perception as regards its aggregate acts, surely that people is blind in respect to justice and to judgment; and, so far from being the repositories of the truth and the faith, it is to them that religion has to be preached: and happy would it be if they could be converted, I will not say to Christianity, but to any religion whatever.

Dr. Goodall, the now venerable head of the American Missionaries in the East, once addressed, in my hearing, some young fellow-labourers, who had just arrived from the other side of the Atlantic, and one of whom had just preached to us a sermon, fervid with prophecy and proselytism, in these terms,—"My dear young friends, you have come here to see practised those virtues we hear of in Christendom."

Before then, it had occurred to myself that the nations of Europe required first to become Mussulmans before they really could be Christians; and in fact, the Christian faith is Oriental, and though the faith be circumscribed to no region, yet its manners and habits are not those of the West. The two social features with which we are acquainted are private charity and international justice. It is to the method adopted practically to maintain both that I attribute more especially the sudden expansion of Islam, its permanency, and the preservation to the present hour of its early simplicity of mind and institutions. I shall now mention the means adopted in respect to the latter.

A special organisation is only intelligible by a due appreciation of the relative functions of the other portions of a state; we must, therefore, first consider in the Mussulman system the regal prerogative, the executive power, and the popular will.

The Prince is the mere executor of the law, but is not possessed of any portion of legislative power, nor of judicial functions. The first he cannot possess, because it is not in exercise at all; the code is immutable, and royal ordinances (the Urf) a mere regulation. As to the second, he is regarded in no other light than as a private individual; he is liable to pursuit before the courts of justice, and there are sultans who have stood to plead their own cause before the tribunal of a cadi. The executive authority is in his hands, but it is limited in every respect as our governments are in some respects — they are most strictly controlled in home matters by Act of Parliament. A Mussulman executive is equally limited by the law in foreign matters. But the law which limits our Governments is a changeable one: they are members of the legislative assemblies, and dispose of the powers of the monarch in his legislative functions; they dispose equally of the influence of Government as of the party which has raised them to power in enacting or in abrogating laws; in obtaining acts of indemnity, or in dispensing even with that protection in cases of their violation of positive law. A Mussulman Government has no such hold, and possesses no such power.

In the West, the opinion of the people constitutes itself a strength and an authority; its will becomes law, and the exercise of that will is called freedom. In the East there is no such thing as opinion; the process of teaching of the whole people corresponds with that which we give to lawyers, and consequently, when commotions break out, it is not with the view of changing institutions, or introducing reforms, but of resisting violence and wrong, and maintaining the law: it therefore ends with the deposition of a sovereign, or the execution of a minister of state; and so, instead of shaking the stability of the throne or of the institutions, serves to maintain them. Consequently the abuses of Government, even in the worst times, though they may prostrate the well-being of a nation, never destroy its common sense, its just appreciation of right and wrong, or its faculty of restoration; for it suffers only from the temporary violence of man, not from the disembodied and undying perversions of legislation.

In the centre of an Administration so simple and patriarchal, is placed the body into whose hands is exclusively remitted the right of judgment on such cases as involve the drawing of the sword. It is, so to say, the Church to which alone this power is intrusted. I use the word "Church," as it is the nearest approach which our language affords; but it also includes the "Bench." Islam is without a priesthood. The doctors of the law are the doctors of divinity, because the law is the Koran: but they are not supported by tithes; their functions are not sacerdotal, but judicial; yet are they a corporation by affiliation, succession, cohesion, wealth, dignity, connexions, and influence—no less authoritative than the Church in England; with this difference, that there is no dissent. Their wealth is derived neither from church property, nor from tithes, nor from state pensions. They are supported by judicial fees on litigated cases, amounting to $2\frac{1}{2}$ per cent, and by the revenues of lands appropriated to the mosques; in the same manner that, amongst the Greeks, lands were attached to the temples. This property is, in consequence, discharged from taxes to the state, and secure against confiscation; consequently, in the political uncertainty of the last two centuries, a large proportion of the property of the Ottoman Empire has been placed in this condition, a portion of the proceeds being secured to the families of the original owners, the remainder entering the treasury of the Efkaf Naziry. The Christians profit by this allocation even as much as the Mussulmans, and at the present moment almost the whole of the property of the city of Constantinople belongs either in this form, or positively by having fallen in, to the body of the Ulema, and pays no taxes to the state. This body, although connected with the aristocracy of the land, and filling the highest administrative offices, has, nevertheless, its roots in the people—resembling, in this respect, the Church of Rome. It is looked up to by the nation, in times of difficulty and danger, as its protector and representative. Every commotion has been led by it, and none has succeeded, except where it has pronounced itself decidedly in its favour.

Those who desire to become acquainted with the details of its constitution will find them elaborately expounded in D'Ohsson; I confine myself to the general outline.

The chief of the body is the Sheik ul Islam, or Grand Mufti. He is nominated by the Sultan, but he can only choose one of the three highest functionaries: these, again, are nominated by the Sultan, but under a similar restriction; and so progressively downwards, the Sultan always nominating, but only from the eligible persons determined and presented by the hierarchal progression of the body itself. It finally rests upon the students in the different colleges who are raised the first two steps by collegiate degrees.

The Grand Mufti, the Cazaskiers of Anatoly and Roumely, the three Cadis of the first cities, and some other dignitaries, form the supreme council of Ulema, or learned men. Their ordinary functions have reference to their own corporation, but in all extraordinary or doubtful occasions they are consulted by the Government; they are not invited to join the divan, but the case is submitted to them. Thus, for instance, before the measures against Mehemet Ali were adopted they were appealed to, and it was on their fetva itself, rehearsed in the firman, that he was declared an outlaw, or, according to their expression, a "Firmanli." The case is not presented to them in the form of documents to examine, but as a solicitor prepares a case for submission to counsel. It is said, "M. or N. has done so and so. Is his act lawful or unlawful; and if so, what is the penalty?" This is the form in which cases with foreign powers are submitted.

It may be said that this is a very inadequate process for arriving at the truth; that they have before them but an *ex-parte* statement; and that even upon it a purely judicial view will not be taken by persons so intimately connected with the Government. These objections are, doubtless, valid; but we must consider how much there is gained, *cæteris paribus*, on the other side. The Ulema are not merely a body of lawyers, they are a representative one, and a popular one; they will not confine themselves to the case as presented by the Government; their opinions and habits are distinct from those of the Administration; they are not compromised by its anterior steps; they will, consequently, in a case of manifest injustice — and this is the important matter — refuse their fetva, and, of course, the Executive is at once stopped. Of what importance is it in the case of any quarrel to have an uncompromised friend, even to consult with? and the quarrels of nations, even more than those of individuals, arise out of intemperance and irritated self-love. What a restraint upon a Government to know that, after it has made a quarrel, it cannot shelter itself under pending negotiations or royal prerogative! and what a support for the morals and the honour of a people that it has only to draw the sword upon a judicial sentence!

But the functions of the Ulema do not cease, in case of war, with the rendering of a fetva. So soon as the frontiers are crossed a representative of the body is sent to the camp, not only to administer justice in the army, but to watch and report on the proceedings of the general, to prevent his overstepping the limits of legality, to take cognizance of his proceedings with the opposite party, and to sign with him armistices or other documents, which, in fact, without such signature, have no validity. The rare cases in which the Turks have broken faith, have arisen out of the ignorance of their enemies of their constitution. They have never, indeed, presented a *forged treaty* to deceive native princes in India, and to avoid parliamentary pursuit at home; but they have been guilty of delivering invalid documents, as in the case of Rhodes—that is to say, uncountersigned by the representative of the Mufti—and then felt themselves at liberty to violate them. But this aberration is the strongest proof of the value of this legal restraint, showing that it was exercised to repress the worst passions, and directly connecting with the institutions of Islam the high character of honour which is never to be found save acting as a moderator. There is but one instance in which ambition induced the Turkish Government to violate an engagement. The voice of religion was then loudly raised against the outrage, and in the subsequent triumphant progress of the Ottoman forces through Hungary to Vienna, which lay exposed and defenceless, when every temptation of easy victory might have led on with eagle's flight the unresisted squadrons, the troops, discouraged by the denunciations of the Ulemas, and the chiefs paralysed by the same cause, exhibited in their insubordination an example of respect for the moral dictates of religion which is perhaps unparalleled in the military history of Europe. The disasters of the campaign, attributed, of course, to other sources by biographers of the Western heroes, let loose the suppressed indignation of the population of Constantinople; and Mahomed IV., after having occupied the throne for more than forty years, was sent to the Seven Towers, to expiate with his life the resumption of hostilities before the expiration of a truce.

To come to later times:—

When in 1812, by the intercession of England, hostilities were put an end to between Russia and Turkey, it became a matter of astonishment to all Europe that Turkey should forego the prospect or the certainty held out to her by the invasion of Napoleon, of obtaining those ends for which she was in arms at that very moment, and for retaking from Russia the immense tracts of country which Russia had possessed herself of during the previous forty years. It was a conviction of the manifest interests of Turkey on this occasion that probably rendered Napoleon indifferent to the negociations of England at Constantinople, and which proved successful beyond all belief, in consequence, no doubt, of the coincidence of English and Russian intention.* Scarcely was the treaty signed, when, as at that of Carlovitz, Turkey perceived her error; but, her agent having appended his signature, no representations and no advantages could induce her to break

* That at the moment of such peril Russia should obtain the accessions of territory by the Treaty of Bukarest, that England in saving Russia should not have regulated with some idea of justice, or some glimpse of future events, the boundaries between Russia and Turkey, is what might have been incredible, but for the more recent experience. It was in the same year (1812) that England secretly arranged with Russia the dismemberment of Denmark, Norway being given to Sweden, that Sweden might not, at the general peace, reclaim Finland.

her faith. When the news of this treaty reached Brussels, Prince Lieven was there in company with a German diplomatist (Baron Ompteda), actually a representative of a foreign state at the British court. On hearing the treaty had been signed, Prince Lieven gave vent to his satisfaction in terms so strong as to surprise those present. The German minister above referred to observed to him that his rejoicing was rather premature, as a hundred thousand treaties could never prevent even a Christian state from seizing the moment of the entrance of the French on Russian soil for repossessing itself of its lost territory; that, consequently, the treaty could only be a feint to deceive the Russians. Prince Lieven, in the unguarded exultation of the moment, exclaimed, "Little do you know the Turks; the ink of that deed is worth more to us than a hundred thousand men."* In proof that the Turkish Government has always maintained the respect for law, still inherent in the breast of its people, and that inoffensiveness which at once renders it worthy of the esteem of foreign powers and the victim of their intrigues, I select a few passages from different periods of their history.

On their first settlement in Europe they restored the Morea, after capturing it, to the Byzantine

* This incident I had from Baron Ompteda.

Emperor, as lawful possessor. They retained Thessalonica only after its capture for the third time, and then on the grounds of a correspondence intercepted, by which the Emperor had disposed of it to the Genoese. At the Treaty of Belgrade, the Grand Vizier justified his refusal to assent to a proposition of the plenipotentiaries as follows:—"You mistake the nature of the Turkish Government. It is not in its power to do things which that of Vienna can do of its own pleasure. It has to consult its people, and it is guarded by a law which it cannot infringe. It partakes of the nature of a republic, and does not wield despotic power."

Sitting with some soldiers at a bivouac fire, one of them was recounting how, at the opening of the campaign of 1828, the perfidious Muscovites had established themselves on the Turkish territory, and were pushing their works up to a small fort where he was in garrison. On which I asked how they could be such fools as not to attack and drive them back. He answered, "War had not been declared." I laughed. Upon this, he leaped up and ran for his musket. I thought he was going to use it against me, but he kissed the stock and said,—"God puts this in my hand, and I will not use it save with His blessing."

It was a similar feeling which led to the destruction of the Turkish fleet at Navarino. They might have annihilated that of the allies as it entered, but they allowed them to take up their positions, waiting till they had fired the first shot.

The classical scholar will no doubt have already been reminded of Rome. There the Ulema was the Fecial College. The Consuls, the Senate, and the People could declare no war; that matter was remitted to the Fecials; and the very negociations with a foreign state were remitted to the legal body, which drew up the *petitio rerum*, transmitted the *ultimatum*, and sent their heralds to the capital of the foreign state to *denounce* the war, remaining thirty days on the frontier before the *ultima ratio* was appealed to and the legions suffered to cross. They threw open the temple of Janus to publish at home the event, so that every precaution should precede, every form of law accompany, and every publicity declare the solemn event. Thus it was that in a Roman the characters of soldier and of citizen were combined, and that discipline and honour were not divorced. Thus is was that the Republic became mistress of the world, and that *Roman* will be a title of honour to the latest generations.

I have contrasted, as antithetical, the legal character of Islam and of the British Constitution. I spoke, however, in respect to the last, not of its ancient principles, but of its present practice. England adopts the law of Rome, and in it the law of nations. It has the Fecial code: *petitio rerum, ultimatum, denunciatio belli,* are still terms of her jurisprudence,—are still legal documents requisite in every such transaction. The Chancellor of England is the great Fecial. The proclamation of war is made in Chancery; it is not a matter settled in a Cabinet Council, for England's law knows neither Cabinet Council nor Secretary of State. England's law knows no more of diplomacy than did the law of Rome; it no more entered into the conceptions of the founders of the one State than of the other to settle such matters by whispers, to maintain normal intrigues amongst other nations, or to suffer them amongst themselves. When a case did arise, then was it judicially decided upon at home; and then was an ambassador expedited to the adverse party *pro hâc vice.*

The founder of experimental philosophy has left us, in regard to politics, a legacy which has long lain dormant. His rule for the rectification of errors in this branch is,—" Stand upon the ancient ways." If this had not been the ancient way, what discovery so great as its invention?

The practical value of the knowledge of other people is the rectification of errors or abuses at home: if we find sound principles and useful habits in a system which we despise, and amongst a people to whom we consider ourselves superior, our pride and prejudice afford additional arguments for such an adoption. This motive has influenced me in the foregoing sketch. I have hoped that the contrast would not be unavailing to open the eyes of my countrymen to this fatal perversion of modern times, which, if not rectified before it be too late, must, according to my judgment, end in the extinction of this Empire, after inflicting incalculable woes on the human race.

Notes of the Editor to the foregoing Essay.

This Essay was written in 1833, and some additions made to it in the few succeeding years, so that it has not been revised since some twenty years ago.

Pp. 163 and 166.—From the following extract from Condé's "History of the Arabs in Spain," it would appear that Islam was offered as an alternative by which war might be avoided. In 963, the King Alhakem declared the obligations of the Muslims when they go on the jihad, or in maintaining frontiers, in this order of the day (given at Toledo):—" It is the duty of every good Muslim to go to the jihad, or war against unbelievers, enemies of our law: the enemies shall be invited to Islam, except when they, as on this occasion, begin the invasion: in the other case it shall be proposed to them either to become Muslims or to pay the established tribute, which the unbelievers under our government have to pay. If in the strife the enemies of our law should not be twice as many as the Muslims, the Muslim who should fly from battle would be vile, and sins against the law and our honour. In entering the enemies' country, kill no women and children, nor the old men without strength, nor the monks of secluded lives, except if they should do you an injury. Neither kill nor take prisoner him to whom you have given a safe-conduct, nor break the conditions and agreements made with them. The safe-conduct which any leader has given, *let all maintain it* .... The leaders shall use their discretion in recompensing those who serve with the army, though not fighting men, or *though of another faith* .... Let none come to the army or to the frontier who have father and mother, without the permission of both of them, unless in case of sudden necessity, when the chief duty is to hasten to the defence of the land, and at the call of the frontier governors." — Chap. 89.

" Some of the Christians of Galicia solicited the king to declare war against other Christians, and many of the Vizirs of the Council and frontier governors desired an occasion for a rupture, knowing that the Christians were carrying on war amongst one another: but the King Alhakem answered them with those words of God's Book,—'Be faithful in keeping your agreements, for God will require an account of them from you.' "— Chap. 90.

P. 177.— It is difficult to account for the origin of this mistake; the " Arabian Nights" are full of contradictions of it, and many Arabic books on religion end with a statement that they are for the benefit of the Muslims and the Muslimahs. Besides, travellers must have observed women going to the mosques.

P. 177.— The differences between the Sunnys and Shiahs are almost entirely political and national: what religious differences there are between the two rites are not the cause of their hostility. The Shiahs are Persians, for there are no Shiahs except in Persia, or where Persians have been. The hatred of the Persians to the Khalif Omer, and their habit of cursing his name alone of the three Khalifs whom they reject, is a remnant of Gheber feeling, or national irritation against the Arab general-in-chief, whose armies subdued their country. This national feeling might have died out if it had not been revived for political objects by Shah Ismail into a national feeling against the Turks. About the year 1200 Persia was overrun by those Turkish bands, from fear of whom the poet Saady " left his home and fled away;" and to this day the greater part of the Shah's subjects speak Turkish rather than Persian. Shah Ismail saw the progress of the Ottoman Turks, and that, on account of the majority of his subjects being Turks, Persia was likely to merge into the Ottoman Empire. He therefore set up the Shiah rite as a device to give a Persian nationality to the Turks within his frontiers; and by making religious distinctions between them and the other Mussulmans, he prevented their looking upon the Ottoman Sultan as the Commander of the Faithful. There were rafizys, or rejectors of the first three Khalifs, before his time, but they differed less from the other Mussulmans; they were few in number, and have disappeared from places where they formerly existed.

The Shiahs in India are descendants of Persians, and there are some others who were brought over to the Mussulman faith by Persians. It is hardly necessary to say that there is no schism in the four Sunny rites, which are equally orthodox, and only differ in the interpretation of small legal points.

P. 178.—It is surprising that writers should continue to charge the Arabs with the destruction of the *Library of the Ptolemies*, when it is well known that it was burned, with its four or seven hundred thousand volumes, during a military operation of Julius Cæsar. It is the more surprising, since Gibbon has thrown doubt on the story, on account of its own improbability and the absence of contemporary authority for it, either Christian or Mussulman; and has said that, even " if " the ponderous mass of Arian and Monophysite controversy were indeed consumed in the public baths, a philosopher may allow with a smile that it was ultimately devoted to the benefit of mankind." The statement that the library was burned by the Arabs was never made till 600 years after the khalifate of Omer, when the Jacobite Christian, Gregory Abulfaraj of Malatia, revived the old story, and transferred it from the time of Julius Cæsar to that of the Arab conquest. Whilst Abulfaraj, in his history of the Sixth Dynasty, speaks less concisely than is usual to him of Cæsar and Cleopatra, and dwells on her love of science, and on the labours of Photinus, the arithmetician and geometrician, who adorned the end of the reign of the Ptolemies, he excludes all mention of the destruction of the library at that time, in order to transfer the story in such a manner as to gratify his feelings against the Arabs. He had also a bias in favour of his own sect, and mentions other Jacobites; and in his story of the library seems to have been desirous of giving prominence to Johannes Grammaticus, also a Jacobite, whom he represents as having asked Amr Ibn ul As for the books in the *Royal* Library. Moreover, the words attributed to the Khalif Omer only stand upon the authority of Abulfaraj, who quotes no testimony in support of them; and they seem like a recollection and travesty of the words of Seneca with regard to this event.

"Onerat discentem turba, non instruit: multoque satius est paucis te auctoribus tradere quam errare per multos. Quadringenta millia librorum Alexandria arserunt . . . . . Non fuit elegantia illud aut cura, sed studiosa luxuria . . . . . Vitiosum est ubique, quod nimium est." Cæsar only says,—" Eodemque tempore, quæ consueverunt navigia per pontes ad incendia onerarium emittere, ad molem constituerunt." And further on,—" Regem cohortatus ut parceret patriæ . . . . . quæ turpissimis incendiis et ruinis deformata esset." This is a case in which it is necessary to "Render to Cæsar."

But supposing it to be true that the Saracens did burn the Alexandrian Library, how can this be made a charge by those who evinced no indignation at the burning of the Summer Palace, and the far greater loss sustained by that destruction of ancient monuments and uninterrupted records of the Chinese Empire?

P. 178.—"The Arabs showed the same tolerance, or still

greater, in the other countries under their rule. They had allowed the Sicilians the free exercise of the Christian religion; they even permitted them to make public processions." (Johannes de Johanne. *Codex diplom. Siciliæ*, quoted by M. Libri.)—*Viardot*, vol. ii. p. 21.

In how many Protestant countries are Catholic processions permitted?

Pp. 184 and 186.—That the abuses of administration are capable of remedy, has been proved by their having been remedied by Sultan Murad IV., in consequence of the memorials addressed to him by Kutchy Bey, remonstrating against the abuses of the administration, particularly with respect to the disposal of the Timariots and Spahiliks to unfit persons, and the great increase of the palace officials and servants. The good effect of Sultan Murad's reforms lasted for some time. One of Kutchy Bey's maxims in his remonstrance against bribery and corruption deserves mention, as being in advance of the age, which seems to favour an opposite idea:—
" Cursed is he that gives as well as he that takes a bribe." As most of Kutchy Bey's writings would apply to the present time, and might again do good service, they were printed lately as a pamphlet, from one of the rare manuscript copies, and are now in general circulation at Constantinople.

The following extract contains an answer to another charge frequently made:—" Reprocher à l'Islam, à la doctrine de Mahomet, la décadence, peut-être irrémédiable, où sont tombées les nations qui la pratiquent aujourd'hui, serait une injustice souveraine. La religion d'un peuple n'a pas avec sa puissance politique de relation directe, absolue et forcée. Autrement en lisant l'histoire des Romains, il faudrait donner la préférence au paganisme, qui vit s'élever la fortune et la grandeur de Rome, sur le Christianisme qui vit sans les empêcher sa chute et sa ruine. Le Koran, au contraire, a donné l'impulsion des conquêtes et de la civilisation à des races indolentes, vieillies dans une immobilité séculaire, qu'il fallait retremper et rajeunir."—*Viardot*, " *Histoire des Arabes d'Espagne*." Paris, 1851. Vol. i. p. 49.

V.

THE GREEK AND THE RUSSIAN CHURCHES.

(WRITTEN IN 1852.)

ANY description of these bodies would no more represent the use to which they are applied, than a sketch of the figure of a chess-board convey the interest of a game. I can only pretend to give the naked outlines, from which the utmost benefit that can accrue may be the dispelling of some vulgar errors, and the indication of some of the obstructions presented to Russia from a quarter which is supposed to afford her only facilities and instruments.

If a Seminole philosopher were detected teaching his fellow-countrymen that Louis Napoleon had great chance of subjugating the Highlands of Scotland because he was the intimate friend of the Pope, who was the head of the Christians, and that the Highlanders were the most religious people belonging to that community, he would be but conveying to the Red Men of the New World a species of instruction very analogous to that which the White Men of the Old World receive respecting Russia, her designs and her instruments. There never was a more gross imposition than the representation of the Emperor of Russia as being Head of, or even in communion with, the Church of the East. The Church—if I can so prostitute the word—of Russia stands, in reference to the Church of Constantinople, as the English Reformation does to the Church of Rome; or would do if, in addition to denying the spiritual authority of the Pope, it substituted for High Priest, or for God, the King or Queen of England for the time being. Supposing such to have been the character of the Reformation in England, what would have been said of the Queen of England interfering to protect the Protestants of France? And supposing that England should, by any extraneous circumstances, grasp at the dominion of Europe, would not the danger arising from her ambition be infinitely greater for the communities of Protestants, from whom she would require the surrender of their faith, than for Catholics, from whom she could only wrest political supremacy?

This hypothesis is the state of the case in reference to Russia and the Greek Church. The proposition strikes directly at every received opinion. I boldly enunciate it, with the view of provoking inquiry and criticism in regard to the proofs I shall adduce. I speak with certain and perfect knowledge of the dispositions of every Christian community in the East, and in what I shall have to state I express their sentiments. I do not mean to say that such will be the answer they will give to a traveller's inquiry, but such they will avow when there is no reason for distrust and no opportunity for deception.

The Church of Constantinople separated itself from that of Rome under Photius. The metropolitan church of Kiof, the daughter of Constantinople, became the primate and mother of the churches of Russia; but, from the ninth century, Constantinople became the Rome of the East, and its spiritual authority remained undivided. The endeavours of the Popes never ceased to reunite Constantinople; and when the Byzantine emperors were endangered by the progress of the Turks, they sought, by reconciliation with Rome, to purchase the military support of the Western Christians. But the Greeks detested the Azymites more than they dreaded the Mussulmans; and the fall of Constantinople may, in a great measure, be referred to these weak endeavours to coerce the consciences of the people. The Greeks of the present day do not hesitate to acknowledge this truth, and even hold the Turkish conquest to have been a special interposition of Providence for the maintenance of the true faith.

At the time that Kiof became the religious metropolis of Russia, it was in like manner the political metropolis. The line of its princes was that which succeeded ultimately in uniting the dukedoms; and as they proceeded to incorporate and to extend their power, their seat was successively transferred to Vladimir and Moscow, in the centre of the proper Muscovite race.

The geographical structure of this region facilitates, to a degree unknown and inconceivable elsewhere, the institution of slavery. Mountains are, in our minds, always associated with freedom; but the contrary idea is not connected with plains, because the Kirghis and the Bedouin, the freest of tribes, live on plains, or wander over steppes: but those plains in the centre of which are placed Vladimir and Moscow, differ from the others in soil and in climate. The wastes of Arabia and the steppes of the Kirghis are not fitted for tillage; they present a scanty subsistence for flocks and herds; there are no cities, and no fixed habitations; the people roam and circulate rather than dwell; they are hardy and enterprising, and rendered by nature bold and free. The products are not such as to render despotism profitable, and the children of the soil are not such as to render it possible. A people of tents is a people of nature; institutions are simple, and men sharp-witted. They can no more be overreached than over-awed by a governing system.

The plains of Muscovy are a rich alluvial soil; the people is, consequently, essentially agricultural and fixed. The dead level of the land is paralleled by an equally deadening uniformity of circumstances; the body is inured to toil, and the mind immersed in torpor. The productiveness of the soil facilitates the accumulation of riches, and the governing power is unrestrained in its action by physical impediments: insurrection finds no protection in mountain gorges — patriotism no immunity in impassable wastes.

Beyond this there is the long duration of winter; the people, shut up at home, are exposed to the visits of the executive force, travelling by snow almost as easily as by the railway. For their hybernation, preparation has to be made by storing the abundant harvest, that ripens with extraordinary rapidity during the summer months. The granaries are the pledges of the people's fidelity. The Russians have never known the art of secreting grain by burying it in the soil; that unobserved protection of the independence of man under all the great systems of antiquity, and in the East at present. Thus it is that the plains of Muscovy afford a peculiar and natural basis for the erection of despotic power. Of this edifice we have seen the plan laid as a diagram, attempted as an experiment, and obtained as a result. There, the people have neither means of resistance nor opportunity of flight. Like the Egyptians under Joseph, they dispose of birthright against food on a tacit contract renewed every twelvemonth. Elsewhere, the throne of despotism balances on a sword; here, it reposes on the buttresses of hunger and cold. One support alone remained to popular rights—the Church. That support too vanished, when the centre was transferred to this cradle of subjection from amongst the pastoral and patriarchal tribes of the South, ennobled and humanised by association with the friendly horse and the dutiful camel. Amongst populations themselves reduced to the condition of beasts of burden, and inured to unvarying and cheerless toil, servitude must be religious no less than political. The Church so transplanted has lost its franchises and its rights—its faculty of defending the people or itself. In the early contests between Rome and Constantinople, Kiof had endeavoured to escape from the supremacy of either; and in like manner the new Church of Moscow endeavoured to escape from the supremacy of Kiof. These dissensions were comparatively insignificant whilst the Tartar yoke weighed on the land. The

Church was then held in the highest reverence by the Grand Dukes, because it was held in respect by the Tartars; and in fact it served as the protection of the people, and finally became the chief instrument for their emancipation. It consequently rose to a position of the greatest influence and authority. As the power of the Tartars was broken, that of the Church took its place, and the Grand Dukes had no sooner relieved themselves from the former than they applied themselves to undermine the latter; and with this view supported the usurpations of the Church of Moscow.

The first prelate who entitled himself "Metropolitan of Moscow" was Theognost, in 1330, but without denying the supremacy of Kiof. In 1462 the title was first assumed of "Metropolitan of all Russia," on the ground that Kiof had a distinct metropolitan subject to Lithuania.* Under the Grand Duke Basil the Blind, Moscow was erected into a Patriarchate,† on the plea that Kiof and Constantinople had both yielded to Rome.‡ Religious dissensions now became embittered, both by these internal measures and by the reaction of the feuds

---

* Mouravief, "History of the Russian Church," p. 80.

† See note at the end of the Essay.

‡ Isidore, patriarch of Kiof, had attended the Council of Florence.

of the East and of Europe, when a new element was thrown in, in the form of a translation of the Scriptures by the Patriarch Nicon, in which passages bearing upon church government were translated to suit the purposes of the Court, and became the basis of the new system of servile theology. The priesthood, not of Kiof only, but of all Russia, was indignant; many refused to use the volume or permit it to be used: its adoption was enforced by penal laws. This was the first religious persecution in Russia, and the recusants holding to the old faith against the new interpolations were called *Starovirtze*, or "old believers."

Shortly afterwards, Ivan the Third, on the capture of Casan, took the title of "Czar of all the Russias;" a title not of new invention, but of common use from the earliest times, and implying a sacerdotal no less than a religious supremacy. It was under this prince that the seed of the present Russia was sown, and, indeed, that the germ expanded itself. By his marriage with the Princess Sophia, and although she had brothers, he assumed to be legitimate successor to the empire of Constantine, and quartered its arms. She was given to him by the Pope, whom he encouraged in the belief of effecting a reunion with the Eastern Church. He excited Germany by the prospect of the decay of the

Ottoman Power, offering himself as a providential instrument for the accomplishment of its destruction. By the expulsion of the Golden Horde he likewise pretended to the inheritance of the Tartars in the East; and under his successor we find communications opened with India and China. On the fall of Constantinople he gathered in the remnants of that State, and pretended to the headship, for Russia, of the Christians of the East, presenting her to them as their future deliverer.

Under his successor, Ivan the Fourth, great strides were made in the same direction. He extended the limits of Russia by the capture of Astrakan and the subjugation of the Nogai Tartars. He finally extinguished the rights of the free cities, sacking the last of them, Pskof. He reduced the nobles to the lowest condition of servitude, and in his reign, appropriately designated one of terror, every vestige of internal independence was swept away.

Under Theodore, the deposed Patriarch of Constantinople, Jeremiah came to Moscow. He lent himself to an inauguration of the Patriarch of Moscow, and declared his independence of that of Constantinople. This occurred in 1588. Jeremiah received a large sum of money for this service.

Peter having left this Patriarchate vacant (as, of course, to the Czars belonged the filling up of an office they had created), was at last called upon by the chief dignitaries of the Church to fill it. It was then he rose, and striking his forehead with his fist, uttered the memorable words, " It is here that there is for you a Master, a Patriarch, and a God." On this he himself officiated at the altar.

Thus by a sacrilege was effected the fusion of temporal and spiritual power, and another, Jeremiah, patriarch of Constantinople, was found to give to it such sanction as the venal adhesion of a displaced prelate could afford. These measures affected solely the Church of Moscow, which henceforward came to be designated as Antichrist by a large proportion of the nation that would not conform, including nearly the whole of the populations of the south dependent on Kiof: the distinction was drawn between the *Official Church* and the *True Church*. From that hour the Russian State contained in its breast an immedicable wound; the knowledge of the sufferings endured and the blood shed has, by the system of government, been concealed from the eyes of the rest of the world: but the facts connected with the revolt of Pougatcheff could not be concealed, however much its causes may have been misunderstood. It was a Starovirtzc insurrection, and with the slightest conduct on the part of its leader it must have upset the throne of the Czars.

The Church property was now confiscated; the clergy received pay from the State; a military organisation was given to it; the priests took army rank and received decorations; and the Holy Synod was instituted to discharge functions of the Patriarch under the directions of a general officer. Its duties were now restricted to the inculcation of abject obedience. The Czar, not in his quality of Patriarch, but of Prince, was declared the Vicegerent of God upon earth; his name was printed in the same form as that of God the Father and of Christ, and his subjects were taught that virtue and religion consisted in the sacrifice of their substance and their lives to the fulfilment of his decrees. The oath administered to the army was not, as with the rest of the world, to obey lawful orders and to *defend* the frontiers, but to obey every order and to *extend* the frontiers. This superstition was not, as in similar cases (if there be a similar case) of human corruption, engendered by oppression, but based on imposture; it was proposed and accepted as a means of advancing the pretensions put forward by Ivan the Third to the succession of Rome in the West, and of the Tartars in the East. The Russian Church is not Erastian, in the sense of sanctioning acts of government; it invests the governing power with the ecclesiastical attributes, transferring to the chief of the State even those of the Lord of the Universe. It does not trouble itself with psychological disputations respecting emanations of the Divine Essence and its manifestations in the flesh. A Czar is not a living Buddha, adored on account of a supposed spiritual abstraction; but the Czar, as a monarch, and because reigning, is the centre of faith and the object of worship; believed in for what he *does*, worshipped by executing his decrees.*

This is not the first time that such blasphemy has been witnessed. The Assyrian monarchs so seated themselves upon the altar, and required the prostrate nations to worship them, not as one of the humble array of gods amongst whom the Cæsars were enrolled, but as God upon earth. No wonder that the Slaavs should claim affinity with this same people, and that the Russian language should afford this very interpretation of that monarch's name.†

Nor are these pretensions advanced under the secrecy of priestly instruction and of the confessional; they are loudly asserted and ostentatiously proclaimed in the face of Europe, in a work published at St. Petersburg in 1840, and entitled "Civilisation and Russia:"‡—

---

* From Russian Catechism.

† Nebuchadnezzar — Ne bug na da Tzar — *There is no God but the Czar*.   ‡ By Count Gurowski.

"The will of the Emperor is the most literal expression of Divine Order transmitted to the earth, whose Imperial person is recognised as the living head of the State and of the Church, and whose decision no written word of the past can bind."

It might be supposed that a people thus deprived of all incentives would sink into a political sea of mud, and that there would result a condition utterly unresisting, but capable of nothing. However, that wonderful thing, the human mind, is always working out for itself unanticipated results, and, placed in new circumstances, ever develops new features. Political prostration has, by discipline, become military strength; and religious prostration, through fanaticism, is transmuted to ambition. Thus has the Muscovite race, by the deprivation of all the objects which brace the arm of nations, or their spirit to heroic deeds, been filled with an unparalleled energy, and a desire to assert their lordship over the human race. "The Muscovite," says a remarkable writer, "pays himself for his present degradation by the hopes of his future supremacy."

The chief occasion is afforded by the existence of co-religionaries in neighbouring empires, subject, in the one, to the rule of the Mussulman, and in the other to that of the still more detested Catholic. These populations do not know that the Church of

Moscow has denied God and put the Czar in His place. They look, besides, to the Czar as their *political* protector, and are glad to find that he has the support of a Church which they imagine to be identical with their own. What the Russians apply to him as Head of the Church they understand as Head of the Christians; and to them Russia is identified with faith, as in Russia faith is identified with the Czar. The Russian *Church* is announced to them as the Oriental Church, and by it is to be conferred political emancipation. The writer who speaks to the Russians of the will of the Emperor in the words I have quoted, thus addresses himself to the Oriental Church beyond the frontiers of Russia:—

"In the East, as in the West, for the whole communion of the Greeks (*subjects of foreign powers*), for the Serb, for the Armenian, for the Montenegrin, for the Georgian, Russia is the Spiritual Life, the Image of God in her Church, —the Social Life, bringing Emancipation, Regeneration, and Perfection. In the bosom of the Russian Church, Faith has endured united and pure, and it will sustain and re-temper the faculties of humanity. That Church alone, amongst all others, has remained in harmony with Order, Hierarchy, and Government; alone has it preserved its Unity, while all others have lost it."*

Here Russia is presented to them as the personification of the Church; she is there personified as

---

* Count Gurowski's "Civilisation and Russia."

their Church. There the Emperor is visible head of State and Church; that Church and its law are called in to give authority to the living and reigning head, or itself instantly annihilated, for his decisions are not to stand upon any law, or to be bound by any. For the *Greeks, Russia* is to be truth in this world and salvation in the next; all other professions as heretical or infidel. The thousand emissaries of Russia are always repeating the same thing. The Mussulmans are the " Empire of Hagar;" the Catholics profess a "dog's faith." But on the borders of the White Sea (the Mediterranean), where England is chiefly apprehended, the art is peculiarly observable. There there is no rancour of contending creeds: the object is effected by epithets. I have often heard the expression at Constantinople, "Are you Christian or English?" which may equally be interpreted, " Are you Christian or *infidel?*" or, " Are you Russian or English?"

If there were subjects of the Russian Crown who abhorred and repudiated this blasphemy, there were those also who equally detested and abjured the external ferocity and internal prostration with which it was associated. We find both characters in the Starovirtze, adherents of the original faith. They are reformers of the public immorality; they combat the general corruption by their life and conversation.

If an exile is succoured on his path, if a prisoner is relieved in his want, if an accused person is aided in his defence, the helping hand is sure to be that of a Starovirtz. With them have taken refuge freedom and charity, expelled elsewhere from the land; and the apparently triumphant progress of the system furnishes daily increasing occasions for the trial of their faith and the exercise of their benevolence.

They have also their partisans, for they have many favourable who do not belong to their body. These partisans are to be found amongst the burghers of all the cities; amongst the merchants of every class; in all the branches of industry, and even in the army: they are not wanting in the general administration, and they have had a representative in the supreme government. From the comprehensive nature of their tenets, every class and every department may at one time or another be reduced to seek their support, and by the total dissimilarity of their ideas from the opinions of the West, that support has no character of conspiracy. Opposing the present union of Church and State, they are in turn the allies of each of the bodies whom that union may oppress; seeking the restoration of the ancient rights of the Boyars and of the prelates, being opposed to the serfdom of the people, objecting to foreign conquest, they are, so to say, the born protectors of each class as it is oppressed, and a living protest against every violence as it is committed. Being destitute of all character of confederacy, and of all organisation for action, it cannot be compromised into acts which would enable the Government to extinguish it in blood.

There being nothing similar in Europe—there being, indeed, nothing similar to the government, by antagonism to which it subsists—it is but natural that it should have escaped observation. It is equally so that the Russian Cabinet should have taken every care to conceal this its great secret. One of the methods which it has most successfully employed to that end is the publication of works hostile to itself, where every other possible charge is brought save this. I take, for instance, the work of Turghenief, where, through three volumes of vituperation, not a word is said respecting the Starovirtze, and the whole question of religion is excluded, except in the last paragraph, where the truth is entirely perverted.

Russia has also taken care to stock the reading public with materials. There is the work of Mouravief—a general officer in active service—on the Church! This book is a careful adjustment of the circumstances, so as to prevent the past facts from being understood. What I have stated I have learned from refugees in Turkey, not one of whom was acquainted with a European language. From them I have also learnt that the Starovirtze of Southern Russia had prepared a petition to the Czar, praying to be allowed to emigrate into Turkey if not permitted to follow in peace their religion at home.

The Greek Christians of Turkey are indeed themselves Starovirtze; they are under the Patriarchate of Constantinople, and not under that of Kiof: but if the Russian sway were established at Constantinople the position of both would be identical: they actually have become identified by a most extraordinary revolution that has occurred in the last few years, and which has rendered Constantinople the metropolis of the dissidents of Russia.

In treating of the Cossacks, I have shown how they had met the attempts of the Russian Cabinet to assimilate their political administration with that of the remainder of the Empire. This population is the stronghold of the Starovirtze: it was the extinction of that sect that the Government had chiefly in view, and while it showed itself disposed and able to resist administrative innovation, it was judged to be more vulnerable in matters of religion. Between the official and the old Church there was no dogmatic difference; a new profession of faith was not required, and if the one priesthood could be substituted for the other the assimilation was complete. This was then the scheme adopted, and it apparently presented great facilities for execution. Hitherto it had been a constant practice to impose one of the official priests upon a parish, but the result was that the Church became instantly deserted.* It was now resolved to convert the siege into a blockade, and to starve them out by the denial of the offices and consolations of religion. The priesthood of Malo-Russia is recruited from the monasteries of the interior; the Government seized and deported the monks and bishops, especially those of Saratov and Kramenchuk, and enrolling them as a regiment sent them to die in the marshes of Lankeran on the Caspian. As the priests died off the parishes remained without the means of baptism, confirmation, marriage, confession, extreme unction, and burial, and were placed irrevocably between the alternatives of absolute infidelity or submission.

Such was the plight in which I found a Cossack settlement in Turkey, where I first became acquainted with these circumstances. They were exceedingly

* The Emperor looks strictly into these matters. On the occasion of one of his visits he went into a church, which he found crowded, but which on a former visit he had found deserted. On inquiry, he discovered that not one of the congregation belonged to the parish. It having been found impossible to constrain the parishioners, who were Starovirtze, to attend, a congregation was brought for the occasion from a distance.

devout, but had no priest; and when I inquired the reason, they broke out into most vehement abuse of all priests, saying they would as soon see the Emperor himself as a priest in their village.

There were, however, Cossacks high placed in the Turkish Government, who cast about for a remedy. In the first instance, their views extended no further than to the Cossack colonies in Turkey; but circumstances soon gave to them an unexpected development. The Porte entered into their views, and communicated upon the subject with Vienna, which was at that moment very cordial towards Turkey, and where the Porte knew, though the Austrians did not, that this sect existed.

At the same time (1771) that the Kalmuks, the followers of the Dalai Lama, fled to the Yellow Sea, a body of Starovirtze had penetrated into Galicia, where, under the name of Ruthenians, they remained undisturbed and unnoticed till the year 1845, when the discovery of them was made by the Archduke Ferdinand in the centre of his government, with as much surprise as if they had been Red Indians. Troops were sent to drive them out, but, bribing the officers, they gained time to appeal to Vienna. One of their priests, Milaradoff, found access to Prince Metternich, and explained to him the real circumstances of the case. Just at this time the communication above referred to took place with Constantinople, the object of which was the establishment of a Starovirtze Bishopric in the Austrian dominions, as Turkey would not venture on so bold a measure herself. The Austrian Arch-chancellor felt all its importance, and did not refuse his concert, but on the condition that the Porte would find an already consecrated Bishop of the Constantinople Church, who would conform in all points to the Starovirtze faith: in such case the Galician district would be converted into a Bishopric and the Prelate inducted. Such a Bishop was found for the consideration of 200,000 ducats; he was despatched to Vienna, received the Imperial *exequatur*, repaired to his new diocese, and in the month of June, 1846, laid hands on eight priests, consecrating them as bishops, and on three hundred laymen, who had repaired from all parts to await their consecration as priests. The Russian Government was no sooner informed of the step than it addressed indignant remonstrances to Vienna, but it was too late. She demanded the extradition of the refugees; but the new Bishops had repaired to Constantinople, and she was constrained to be satisfied with the abolition of the Bishopric (the Bishop was sent in September, under surveillance, to Cylli, in Styria), and the engagement was taken to permit the entrance of no more Ruthenians, and several who have since passed the frontier have been seized and given up.

At the period of the conquest of Constantinople by the Turks, the dependence of the Church of Russia on that of Constantinople was considered by both parties as affording powerful means of action to the Sultan in Russia. What I have before stated would suffice to show, that at that period there was no religious jealousy between Mussulmans and Christians. The Church at Constantinople, far from suffering by the Mussulman conquest, acquired prerogatives and authority such as it had never known under the Christian Emperors. It was interfered with neither in dogma nor in ceremony, and, moreover, power was vested directly in its hands. The priests everywhere became municipal officers; the prelates became judges in many civil and in all ecclesiastical cases; and the Patriarchate was erected into a supreme court for its nation, the sentence of which was executed without pretence to revision, except in capital cases, by the Turkish authorities. It had, moreover, administrative functions, and apportioned the taxes between the provinces. To actual power was added dignity and respect. The conqueror Mahomed II. himself held the stirrup of the Patriarch when he came to visit him. Nothing then was more natural than an alliance of the Church with the Mussulman Government, and the Russian Czar had justly to apprehend the political action of the priesthood sent from Constantinople throughout his dominions. In applying himself to ward off this danger was commenced that system of cajolery, and framed that scheme of perfidy and corruption, which in aftertimes succeeded in reversing upon Turkey those very dangers. But the system has been worked to excess and pushed beyond endurance, so that now the wheel has completely gone round; and the fourth century, at present completed, brings us back exactly to the position of 1453, when the Churches of Russia are supplied from Constantinople with priests whose sympathies are with the Sultan and against the Czar. This is one of the necessities which force Russia into action, and which render the destruction of the Ottoman Empire a condition of her own existence.

The revolution to which I have referred affects indeed but a most insignificant portion of the subjects of Turkey, but circumstances of another kind have alienated from Russia each of the other populations professing the Greek faith. These I shall now pass rapidly in review.

The creation of the official Church in Russia might be conducive to the ends of internal despotism, but that very despotism had itself its end in foreign conquest. The official Church was therefore an instrument forged for the conquest of the Byzantine Empire. By bringing Church and Government into one line, adhesion to the faith became equivalent to allegiance to the Prince. The Patriarch of Moscow was to be substituted for that of Constantinople (possessed by infidels); and when the Patriarch was merged in the Czar, the sovereign of Russia was the legitimate sovereign of the professors of the Greek Church, subject to the usurpation of the Mussulman Sultan. So long as the administration of Russia did not touch those provinces, the suppression of the Church by the State was not observed, and in the disorders of Turkey the Christians naturally turned to a foreign prince, who, in claiming their spiritual allegiance, offered them political protection. Under this illusion the whole country was opened to the propagandism of the priesthood. The Patriarchate of Constantinople fell into the absolute dependence of the Russian Embassy. The Greeks, insignificant indeed by numbers, but of real importance by intrigue, apparent importance, and volubility, invaded all its offices and filled its prelacy. They appeared everywhere as Russian agents and creatures. The 12,000,000 of the Greek Church in European Turkey, of Turkish,* Roumain, and Slaav

---

* The Bulgarians, amounting to about 5,000,000, are of Turkish origin. They were the original Tartars of the Volga, whence they have derived their name.

blood, detested the Greeks as a race; so that the association alienated those populations from Russia. This explains the simultaneous and unremitting endeavours made during the last thirty years by Wallachia, Bulgaria, and Serbia, not to emancipate themselves from the Patriarchate of Constantinople, but from the Greek Prelacy, and to substitute natives for these adventurers. This was effected in Serbia soon after they had acquired their independence. A similar change was made in Bulgaria, as one of the reparatory measures of 1851. It has also been one of the reforms most urgently demanded on the north of the Danube. A change in the constitution of the Patriarchate has ensued, as may have been gathered from the recent declaration in favour of the Sultan against the professed protection of the Emperor of Russia. What a contrast with the parallel case of 1821, when the Patriarch was the first victim of a similar declaration, and was hanged as a malefactor before his own door!

But it may be supposed, that if the other populations were alienated by this preference of the Greeks, the Greeks themselves must have been conciliated. Now the Greeks are far too astute to work for Russia, save for their own individual benefit. No population knows Russia so well; none detest her so thoroughly; none would suffer more by the triumph of the Russians or the fall of the Turks. Their services have been indeed of immense value, but it is only as practising on others: she can use them as local agents, as dragomans at Constantinople, and as Turkish ambassadors in London and Paris, but they are of no service to her whatever as a people; and for this reason, that they do not exist as one: they did so, indeed, in the Morea and the islands, but these are no longer included in the Turkish dominions, and we shall presently see how they stand affected. There is in Thessaly a Greek population, which amounts to about half a million; that is the only one, and even that one did not take part in the Greek insurrection, when every chance was open to it. Elsewhere the Greeks are but shopkeepers, or brokers, or priests. They have no country, they have no cities, they have no mountains, they do not bear arms, they are mere pedagogues or huxters.

I cannot better illustrate the universal defection, in a religious sense, from Russia, than by the Church measures adopted by independent Greece, so soon as that State was constituted on its own basis. Russia, of course, expected to establish there her official Church; it was impossible that it should remain dependent on Constantinople; an independent Church of the Morea was a pretension too visionary for a moment to be admitted; she consequently despatched from Odessa by a frigate, through the Dardanelles, a model sacerdotal establishment, to be set up in the Russian Embassy. The Greeks had, from the very commencement of the War of Independence, been especially jealous of her interference; their first appeal to Europe, through England, was for protection against that interference: they declared through the then minister, Rhodias, that they would rather perish to a man than submit to any conditions dictated by her; they said that they knew her purposes and her perfidy, and preferred to her protection the despotism of the Turks. The same opinions were energetically expressed by Mavrocordato in an anonymous letter, published at the time, in the "Courier de Smyrne." England, however, as usual, forced that protection upon them, enabled the Russian faction to establish itself, and sanctioned for Europe the belief that Russia commanded the affections of the Greeks. With this knowledge there will remain nothing enigmatic in the fact, that the Greeks should resolve to anticipate the plan of uniting them to the official Church by instituting an independent Synod of their own. King Otho had not yet arrived, but his place was occupied by a Regency of four members, one of whom only (Armansberg) was a Russian; the majority, struck by the representations made to them, hastened to pass a law for the creation of the Synod. The exasperation of Russia knew no bounds; the majority of this Regency, constituted by a European treaty, was expelled by violence, troops being landed from the Russian squadron to enforce the decree in case they had offered resistance. As usual, the order came from London, and the pretext that was employed was, that they were "Russians."*

Having thus, I trust, effectually disposed of the revolutionary element afforded in Turkey by religion, in so far as it can be handled by Russia, I now come to the condition of the dissidents internally.

A revolution may be made without any reason, but the religious constitution of Islam never could afford a reason for the revolt of its subjects of another faith. They are, indeed, rayahs; but the condition of rayah is not one of disqualification or dishonour. In point of social etiquette there is a great distinction, but this is one belonging to the

---

* The details of these transactions will be found in the history of the Regency, published by Messrs. Abel and Maurer, two of its members, with the concurrence of General Heidech. Further and confirmatory details will be found in the work on Greece of Professor Thiersch, tutor to King Otho, sent to Greece before him, and whose return to that country was prevented by the order of the English Minister.

habits of the people, and you might as well attempt to attack caste in India. The Mussulmans are a superior caste: they have become so practically, not having been so by the original constitution, for to this day those social distinctions do not exist between Arabs of different creeds. The Christians, as Churches, possess in Turkey privileges unknown to any Church in Europe, whilst in religious matters the congregation is in possession of rights of which they have been deprived in Christendom. Here alone is to be seen to-day the constitution of the Apostolic times; here the flock elects the pastor, and the Sultan confirms invariably the election: no monarch has ever usurped, from either the consistory or laity, the nomination to bishoprics; and no King or Pope by Concordat has disposed of them to each other. The Christians may, in evil times, have been subject to misrule and to oppression, but it is not as Christians that they have suffered; when animosity has been aroused against them by acts of foreign power, or their connexion with them, again they have suffered as traitors, not as Christians.*

* An Instruction of the Propaganda, in 1849, to the Lebanon, explained for the guidance of priests in the confessional that acts which would be criminal against a Christian King are not less so against a Mussulman Sultan.

Men are not by nature informed and wise, and it does not follow that a people should be content because it has reason to be so. Men may enjoy benefits without knowing them, and, still more, be ignorant of contrasts which would make them doubly dear. The Christians of Turkey are not aware that they enjoy the benefits of toleration, because they have never belonged to a European Government; they do not know that they have the benefit of being free from taxation to a dominant Church, nor that they have the enjoyment of any privilege in the fact of electing their pastors: the clergy are not aware that they are in possession of singular power in their judicial and administrative functions; but how is it that Europeans do not see those things? How is it that they do not enlighten them regarding these contrasts? However, there are those who are neither caught by such fallacies nor backward to expose them. In a controversial work against the Church of Rome, published at Constantinople in 1850, the most learned of the modern Greeks writes as follows:—

"In reference to the charge brought against us of our being subject to the august descendants of Osman, 'whose political influence,' according to M. Villereau, 'has entirely swallowed up the ecclesiastical power,' we may remark that the Ottoman Government does not in the least degree prejudice our religion; neither has it, indeed, at any time up to the present day, in any way injured it. Every nation is under the obligation of submitting, after God, to a temporal power.

* * * *

"Our Government grants us freedom of worship and the public performance of our rites, and secures to us the enjoyment of these privileges through the political authority with which it has invested the Patriarchs and Archbishops.

"The internal administration of the Church has at no period been interfered with, the election of the four Patriarchs and of their bishops having ever been freely made by their own synods. The career of religious instruction lies open to the holy ministers, and even the schools for public instruction enjoy the patronage of Government. If at times, and in some places, far from the centre of administration, or in the midst of troubles, unruly men have raised their barbarous hands upon churches and schools, the Government, as soon as apprised of such occurrences, has remedied the evil and punished the guilty.

"The celebration of divine worship in our holy temples is performed with so much pomp, that a Carmelite monk, nearly two hundred years ago, after being present at one of our ceremonies, expressed his admiration as follows:—'On the 4th of January, 1679, I was present, in the name of Mr. De Nointel, during the celebration of mass by the Patriarch Dionysius at Constantinople. I cannot imagine that anything more imposing and magnificent could have been exhibited on this day, even in the most flourishing times of the Greek Church.'

"Were we to be so presumptuous as to pry into the wonderful and inscrutable decrees of Divine Providence, we might discover that the preservation of the Orthodox and Catholic Church was secured through the downfall itself of the Roman Empire. For who does not at once perceive that ultimately the Orthodox remnant would have been rent in twain by those unfortunate sovereigns who, listening to the suggestions of the Pope and other European Governments, saw no hope of preserving their power save by apostasy, and by abjuring the orthodox, the catholic, and the apostolic faith of their forefathers; they contrived to maintain themselves for a short time by gradually corrupting that Church, and by the appointment of Patriarchs, such as the fraudulently elected Beccos, and Gregory the pseudo-Gennadius? Who does not see that this must have continued whichever of the Western Powers had obtained the ascendancy? Were it not that the narrative would cast ignominy on the name of Christian, and had I paper to waste and time to spare, I might, from the materials of Frank historians themselves, revive the recollection of the many and furious persecutions, the coercive measures, exiles, imprisonments, tortures, martyrdoms, which our immortal forefathers had to endure, whenever the Papal rule under the cloak of a Michael or a Beccos, or the Frank Crusaders, especially in Syria, Cyprus, Crete, and even at Constantinople under Cardinal Pelagius, prevailed; and thus point out the tyrannical violence with which the Pope's blessing hand was used for the destruction of Orthodoxy.

* * * *

"Shortly before the fall of Constantinople the Pope's emissary assured the distracted Constantine, who had emplored his aid, that this would be granted on condition of his receiving again Gregory Mummus, whom he had expelled for professing Latin doctrines. At this critical emergency, when both the Emperor and his people, reduced to the last extremity, were on the verge of renouncing their faith, the interposition of the sharp-edged sword of the invincible Ottomans was evidently providential. It cut asunder at one blow, and for ever, the chain which impiety had cast around the neck of the Church professing orthodoxy—the Church which on this occasion washed off by her martyrs' blood, whatever stains or defilements had polluted her in her contact with the temptations of heresy; and now rejoices in presenting herself before God, 'purified, holy, immaculate, having neither spot nor wrinkle.'

"The throne of Constantinople had become by heresy a snare unto the feet of religion: how, then, should not every one of the faithful exclaim with the Psalmist, 'The snare is broken asunder and we are delivered. Our help is in the name of the Lord!' For this it is we do praise, and must ever praise, with thanksgivings, the Almighty, who has provided us with, not as M. Villereau would have it, 'a scourge,' but in reality with a severe master, but a faithful guardian—the Ottoman Government, which proved instrumental in cutting off every connexion between us and the nations of the West, and thus effectually preventing the corruption which threatened our immaculate religion."— Παπιστεριῶν Ἐλέγχων, tom. i. p. 245.

The same writer, speaking of the constitution of the Church, thus proceeds:—

"The conqueror and his illustrious successors, down to the present Sovereign, have invariably invested the persons of the Patriarchs with plenipotentiary dignity whenever the constitution interferes with religion, or even religion with the constitution. Likewise legislators and expounders of the law are of opinion, that the *Sheriat-i-Sheriff* in sundry cases, such as matrimony, affinity by marriage, inheritance, when it decides differently from the law of the Christians and the precepts of the Gospel, or the maxims of the Apostles, shall not be enforced, in order not to wound the consciences of the Christian subjects, whose liberty of worship is declared inviolable; and they therefore invested their spiritual pastors, such as Patriarchs and Bishops, with the power of pronouncing judgment, and so punishing the disobedient and unruly."

I have now to point out a recent infraction of those ancient and venerable institutions; but the incident, however it may affect the future fate of Turkey, confirms what I have said respecting its character. It has deviated from its rules, but it is a rule from which it has deviated; the deviation has sprung neither from pride nor from pretension, but from weakness, and the crime has been imposed by the powers of the West. What I am about to relate ought to be easily apprehended by Englishmen, since it is no other than a similar act to that which was designated a Papal *Aggression*, by which this great empire was for the space of a year agitated, distracted, and convulsed.

A Papal rescript, similar to that of 1850 for England, partitioned the Catholic Armenians into six Bishoprics, appointing Bishops thereto. Turkey, like England, submitted, but only in consequence of the coercion applied to it by the French Government: but observe the difference of sense of the people; the usurpation of the Pope was not denounced by the Mussulman as an attack upon the sovereignty of the Sultan, and it was not received as a boon by the Armenians. The Sultan resisted it as an oppression of his Catholic subjects, and the Armenians resisted it as an usurpation on their own rights. There was no animosity between Christian and Mussulman; no

Grand Vizier published inflammatory letters; no ministry was displaced; no absurd or inoperative bill was carried for a prerogative that never was touched, and the injured party was not left at once unprotected and vituperated; no greater triumph was given to the Pope, beyond all his other triumphs, in a triumph over the mind and the divan of Turkey.* The difference of this common sense resulted from the natural position in which the Christian Churches in Turkey stood, and from their possession and exercise of ancient and immemorial rights. No man could there be deceived with reference to the nature of the Pope's rescript; it was clearly the abrogation of the right of the community to nominate its own religious officers, and the subversion of their corporate authority. Who, then, could have imagined that a regulation touching titles could affect the wrong, or touch the matter in any way at all? Who could be so insane as to suppose that the Sultan's authority was compromised therein, except in so far as that a particular class of his subjects might be injured?

A Roman Catholic Bishop in Turkey does not stand in the same position as one in England; he is not a nominee of a foreign priest whom the Government does not choose to recognise, but being the elected of the people and their administrator he

---

* Words of Lord John Russell altered to the case.

becomes thereby a functionary of the Crown. The Porte has no Concordat, and no treaty with the Pope, but it does not say—" Do what you like with your spiritual subjects for I do not profess your faith;" but it says to its subjects—" Write to the Pope what letters you like, and read, if you are disposed, what letters he sends; but no prelate is to rule you, except when he has received my firman of investiture, and that firman is granted only on your own election." Consequently, the rescript of the Pope fell just as dead a letter as if it had constituted so many pashalics or nominated so many pashas. But when the French Government was known to press the matter, and it was apprehended that the Porte would yield, the Armenians interposed by petition, praying that the firman might not be granted. France, however, persevered. Simultaneously a fictitious quarrel was got up between her and Russia, on the subject of the Holy Sepulchre; the instruction to M. Lavalette, received from the Pope himself, was to yield on the latter question and to press the former. The Russian Government, who certainly had as much interest in the one as in the other, drops the one and presses the other. England then, in the midst of the full frenzy of its "Papal Aggression Bill," recommends a "temporising policy;" that is, submission; or, in other words, the granting of a firman, which would have been equivalent to the inducting by Royal ordinance of Cardinal Wiseman as Archbishop of Westminster. But all this would not have sufficed unless an Armenian Primate (Artim Bey), to whom that people had entrusted its care, and who belonged to the hollow system of Egypt, had at the last moment turned round, misleading the Porte by that very authority entrusted to him to oppose the measure. Thus was extorted this fatal concession, not by infatuation and fanaticism, but by art and intrigue, in which Russia nowhere appears, having her work done for her, as usual, by her miserable tools. Turkey may arouse the fanaticism of her Christian subjects, but it is only in so far as she yields to the threats and counsels of her European protectors, or degenerates into a resemblance with them of character and infatuation. The following letter from a Roman Catholic ecclesiastic, often referred to in the discussions on the Papal Bill, cannot fail to be read with interest:—

"Lavalette came, before going to Constantinople, to receive his instructions from His Holiness, and though there were the two questions, that of the Bishops and that of the Holy Places at Jerusalem, the first was considered the one of importance. His means of carrying it were at that time Artim Bey, the very man upon whom the adversaries of the Bishops relied!

"The clergy will now see the avenues of preferment

closed against them, and will be reduced to dependence on a distant court, and from it solicit all favours through the French Ambassador or Archbishop. If this were but a solitary phenomenon it would be deplorable; but how much more so when it is one of a series of measures tending to destroy throughout the world, in the Catholic clergy, all freedom of action and all spirit of independence, placing them under the direct management and direct nomination of the Propaganda!

"To Turkey this is peculiarly dangerous, as she has no representatives to watch the manœuvres of the powers who direct the movements of Rome. It has hitherto been the policy of the Porte to prevent its Catholic subjects from being subject to foreign interference; and who could have dared to press it against so triumphant a reason for its refusal as this,—'We only give firmans for Bishops on the solicitation of their future flocks?' For a whole year the Armenians rejected the solicitations of the Pope to ask for this firman, and now comes an Ambassador, not from the Pope but from France, and the firmans are delivered. It might prevent much evil if all correspondence with Rome were carried on through a member of the Divan—the great majority of Catholic prelates would hail such a decision. The Catholic Patriarch of Antioch was only prevented from making such a proposal last year by apprehensions of the vengeance of the Propaganda. Any power that now wishes to use that population of the Turkish Empire has only to purchase the Secretary of the Propaganda, and venality in that quarter is not unheard of.

"The Porte may retrace its steps—it may, for the future, insist upon the Pope's respecting the ancient privileges of the Armenian nation in the election of their own Bishops. When it consented at the Pope's request, more than twenty years ago, to withdraw a large number of the Armenians from the authority of the Primate of Constantinople, it could not mean to establish over them an absolute master and a foreign head, who might be but a puppet in the hands of enemies. The Pope has a right to confirm the election of a Catholic Primate; but here his ancient jurisdiction, except in appeal, ceases. Let the Porte secure to the national clergy and people the liberty of canonical election, which up to the present time they have always enjoyed, and it will not only ensure the unbounded devotion to the Sultan of the Catholic Armenians, but it will ere long see them joined by large numbers of the religious subjects of the Russian Catholics of Utchmiadzin."

This measure was followed by a Papal rescript to the Papal legate of Antoura, in the Lebanon, which is the stronghold of Catholicism in the East; the effect of which would have been to transfer into the hands of the Roman authorities the complete control of the conventual and other religious funds, in a country where a very large proportion of the public property belongs to the convents, which may be considered rather in the light of industrial associations than of ascetics. Here, however, the resistance of the people was successful, and France did not interfere. There are sufficient local grounds to prevent her from attempting it; the ill-will of the Catholic Armenians was to her a matter of no importance: not so the ill-will of the Maronites, which she must have thereby incurred. The Lebanon has always been for her a source of trouble and vexation; it is termed, in the Paris Foreign-Office slang, *la Bouteille d'Encre*. To avoid the recurrence of similar troubles and dangers, the consulate of Beyrout had been removed from the list of political consulates and placed on the commercial, and the *personnel* had been changed to give effect to this alteration. Had the matter been pushed in the same way as that of the Bishops, the Catholic body would have been simultaneously convulsed in every portion of the Ottoman dominions. At the same time the Maronites were exasperated by the measures taken for pushing Protestant proselytism, through the instrumentality of the American missionaries. In the North, the Armenian Catholics threatened to relapse to the old Armenian Church, or to join the Greek; the old Armenian Church is now under the patronage of Russia, and the Greek Church is of course her church.

The Pope, in the plenitude of his power in ancient times, and in the religious freedom of action which he retained till the late revolutions, never attempted such measures as these. In later times the direction of its policy was quite the reverse, and Europe was astonished to behold a legate of the Pope at Constantinople and an ambassador of the Sultan at Rome. I have the best reason for knowing that this was no matter of caprice, but based upon a mutual appreciation and a necessity of common defence: in fact, matters had gone so far that it was a question of instituting a diplomatic college at Rome, and directing the studies of one of the most powerful of the religious corporations to the mastering of the policy of Russia, and to the means of upsetting it; and Rome possessed for this end opportunities, not only immense, but seductive. It might have made itself the director of the Catholic governments; it might have created in both Houses of Parliament in England a body of protectors of English rights and of public honour; and while securing itself against the deadly blows levelled at the faith of Poland, and securing its own station as a Church in opposition to the Greek Church, might have given to itself a claim to the respect and veneration of mankind. The power of Rome would have revived in a new fashion, a moral character conferred upon its action, and an intellectual aim given to its pursuits. No greater danger has menaced Russia in this or in any former age; but then came the revolutions of 1848.

Shortly after these events I met an influential person in the counsels of Rome, who had been one of the most active in promoting the plan above indicated. His first words were these,—" Circumstances are now completely altered ; *we owe everything to the Czar.* In the moment of our distress, with unheard-of generosity, he came forward, and placed his treasury and his army at our disposal. Of course, that kind of succour was out of the question; *but we owe to him the presence of the French.*" On expressing my surprise that he had not perceived the escape that Russia had had, and that he should mistake an insolent triumph for a benevolent act, he answered,—" Oh, we are not deceived; we know that it is out of no love for us: but we are upon the same line—*that of order.*" *

The startling circumstances thus revealed are fully borne out by documents that have been made public. So early as the month of February, 1848, the Cabinet of St. Petersburg thus addressed itself to the Court of Rome:—

"It is beyond doubt that the Holy Father will find in his Majesty the Emperor a loyal supporter in effecting the restitution to him of temporal and spiritual power, and that the Russian Government will apply itself to all the measures that may contribute to this end, seeing that it nourishes in respect to the court of Rome no sentiment of rivalry and no religious animosity." †

---

* Mazzini having been once asked how he could reconcile to himself the pecuniary assistance afforded by Russia to his party, answered,—" There is no love lost between us; we merely happen to be on the same line — *that of disorder.*"

† "Egli è fuor di dubbio che il S. Padre troverà in S. M. l'Imperatore un leale aiuto per farlo ristabilire nel suo potere temporale e spirituale, e che il Governo Russo si associerà francamente a tutti provvedimenti che potranno condurre a queste fine, che esso non nutre verso le Corte di Roma verun sentimento di rivalità ne veruna animosità religiosa."—*Farina,* "*Stato Romano,*" vol. iii. p. 215.

The Papal rescripts for England and Turkey have therefore to be referred to the influence which had now gained the ascendency at Rome; and in consequence of the revolutionary movements which England had fomented: indeed, during the discussions on the Papal Bill, it was on all hands admitted that the aggressions sprang from a political and not from a religious source. The English Prime Minister spoke of a conspiracy acting from Rome and threatening Europe. This was after all the religious topics had been exhausted.* The conspiracy that ruled at Rome was not France, but Russia. She it was who had an object in setting Protestants and Catholics by the ears; she it was who had to convulse Turkey by a religious hatred, and to make the Catholics, no less than the Greeks, turn to her as their sole hope and protection. France's object in protecting the Catholics was to gain influence. Was it to be secured by openly forcing their own Sultan to oppress them? The Pope sought to extend his flock by proselytism. Could he have devised an innovation, the unmistakeable effect of which was apostasy?

* Lord Shaftesbury, in his spoken speech, had already taken the same view. He spoke of the rescript having been dictated by the "bayonets from which the Church of Rome drew its breath;" but all this was cut out of the speech in Hansard, where nothing but "Catholic" and "Protestant" is to be found.

This leads me to a matter as yet unopened, but which ere long may attain, as all others with which we are mixed up, a painful and noxious importance, and that is the union of the Greek and Latin Churches. This, indeed, is an old story, and forgotten in our times; but circumstances have now assumed that shape in which it may one day suddenly be realised.

Whenever the Czars have had a point to carry with the Pope they have flattered him with the hope of conformity—a hope utterly vain, because then the Greek Church would have become Catholic. The altered position of the Pope and Czar would now make the Catholic Church and the Catholic body Russian; the Roman Catholics would no longer then be filled with abhorrence of the chanting of the first Greek mass in St. Sophia, but would be the first to sing hallelujahs or pæans on the event.

If such an idea does exist in the thoughts of the Russian Cabinet, we will doubtless observe traces of it in their conduct, and preparations for its execution. Such symptoms are to be observed, and they are of a nature to render any other explanation difficult.

So soon as the Russian Cabinet had taken its measures to render a revolution in Italy inevitable, the Emperor repaired thither to lay the seeds for the after-game. It was a dramatic performance:

he, the "head of the Greek Church," knelt to the Pope for his benediction; he kissed his hand and ring; he then repaired to St. Peter's, and laid himself at full length upon the tomb. Meanwhile, his Minister narrated to the public the circumstances of the interview; promised the Papal Government every concession in respect to Poland, and used every means, social and diplomatic, to make the Romans believe that the Muscovites were their only friends on earth. One of the avowed organs of Russia meanwhile, following one of her religio-military authorities, pointed out the necessity of a union of Rome and St. Petersburg to combat immorality, infidelity, and Protestantism.

The question of mixed marriages had hitherto been one of the great differences between Rome and Russia, as it had also been with the Protestants. From the month of March, 1848, the Greek Popes abstained from requiring in such marriages the conditions, hitherto rigorously enforced, respecting bringing up the children in the Greek faith. The form in which they expressed themselves was that of deferring the settlement for a year, sometimes remarking, to the surprise of their auditors,—"In a short time we shall all be of one church."

From the same period all persecution has ceased against the Catholics in Russia, and the prelates of that Church have been treated with the greatest consideration and distinction.*

The most significant incident, however, has been the publication of a ukase on the subject of Purgatory, assimilating in that respect the doctrines of the Greek to that of the Roman Church.

To judge of the possibility of such a union, we must turn to those doctrinal points upon which the project has hitherto been apparently shipwrecked, and which have consequently been supposed to present insuperable obstacles: they will be found to be exceedingly tractable.

The first point is the procession of the Holy Ghost. A solemn anathema had been denounced against whoever should add or take away from the creed. The Pope added the "Filioque," and the Greek Patriarch, not denying the doctrine, denied the authority, and declared that the Pope had incurred the anathema. The authority that has prostrated the ancient Russian Church, submitted the prelacy to military discipline, and made a layman chief priest—the Czar to-day—will find no difficulty in introducing the "Filioque" and in raising the anathema.

As regards Purgatory, the objection is rather for

---

* See note at the end of the Essay.

the ignorant than the learned. The Greeks admit prayers for the dead, and thereby recognise a place of durance for the soul. The Latin Church has used the word as expressing St. James's idea of the purifying of fire, which separates the good metal from the dross; while, as the body is not exposed to it, the fire must be metaphorical; and such, in fact, was the declaration registered in the Council of Florence, under Eugenius IV. The recent ukase disposes of the abstraction.

The only other point not purely one of discipline is the Supremacy of the Pope; but all the Pope pretends to over the Patriarch of the East is the appellate jurisdiction, the presidency in general councils, and the right of calling them. The Patriarch of Constantinople yields to him the place of honour, holding him *primus inter pares;* the Patriarch of Moscow, who may be recreated for the nonce, will question neither.

Every other distinction in discipline has already been conceded by the Church of Rome to the members of the Eastern Church who have entered her communion under the name of *United Greeks*, just in the same way as she has adopted the national peculiarities and the original liturgies of the Copts, Jacobites, Maronites, and Armenians. The clergy of the United Greeks are married; the Eucharist is consecrated in leavened bread; the Greek, and not the Latin language, is used in the liturgy; sculpture is excluded from the churches. On the other hand, in the Greek Church, the names of the Popes canonised previous to the separation are venerated as saints, and spoken of as successors of St. Peter; and a Catholic at the hour of death would have no difficulty in sending for a Greek confessor, if a Catholic one was not at hand.

Thus, then, the difficulties of every kind, in so far as doctrine and discipline are concerned, are smoothed down; the advisability of the measure will depend solely upon political considerations. The objection which hitherto prevailed in the independence of the Pope has disappeared, and the union of the Churches would seem to be the recompense of the supremacy achieved at Rome and Vienna. It would be the application to the West of a similar process of disorganisation· to that which has been so long employed in the East; it would be of the most essential importance in the assimilation of Poland, for in the negotiation mutual concessions would be made, and it would be easy thus to obtain the substitution of a Greek for a Roman hierarchy, and of the Greek for the Latin tongue.

The point, however, which we have chiefly to consider is the effect on Turkey; I speak not at present of indirect effects produced through Europe, but of her direct relations with the two creeds. Passing by the period of diplomatic action from a distance, during which the professors of the Eastern Church appear to be, and act, as her partisans, and coming to that of actual possession—a possession which in the first instance would be confined to European Turkey, and which would be accompanied by the retreat into Asia of the Mussulman Turks—let us see in what predicament Russia would then find herself. The suppression of the Mussulman government, the retreat of the Mussulman population, at once sweep away all the grounds of favour which she can possess at the present moment, and every means of conciliation and association which she can use. Down on the native population, taught by herself, filled with the most extravagant sense of its importance and exultation in its triumph, would come the crushing weight and the exasperating features of the Russian administration; instantly the religious question will appear; she would find herself placed between two organisations—the one Catholic, her bitter foe from olden time; the other *Greek*. Here let us pause.

At the period of the Treaty of Kainardji, in 1774, M. de Thugut, then internuncio of Austria at the Porte, addressed to his government a memoir reviewing the treaty and its effects, anticipating, under misapprehensions then universal, the downfall of the Ottoman Empire, in consequence of the religious adherence of the Greek Church to Russia, but, with a discrimination seldom equalled, showing to the Austrian Government that it could compensate for those acquisitions by none on its own part, and that the neighbouring fragments of Turkey which it might incorporate could only hasten its own final subjugation. "Such aggrandisement," he says, "of the Austrian territory would not excite the jealousy of Russia, for those provinces (Bosnia and Serbia) are inhabited almost entirely by Mahomedans and *schismatic Christians:* the former would not be tolerated as residents there; the latter, considering the close vicinage of the Oriental Russian Empire, would not delay in emigrating thither; or if they remained, their faithlessness to Austrian power would occasion continued troubles; and thus an extension of territory without intrinsic strength, so far from augmenting the power of his Imperial Majesty, would only serve to weaken it."

This statement applies to Russia herself: those Christians, "schismatic" to Austria, would be no less schismatic to Russia; if, as the price of their having expelled "the accursed Empire of Hagar," according to the terms of the publication of the

Holy Synod of Moscow, they were required to receive the Emperor as Vicegerent of God upon earth, and to acknowledge as Patriarch a General Officer and his colleagues, they would very soon remember not only that the Mussulman Caliph had imposed neither serfage nor conscription, but that he respected the name of Christ and honoured His people, their priests and prelates. With the fickleness which we must admit as the cause of the event which we contemplate, they would soon invite a Sultan from Broussa or Iconium, as they had invited a Czar from Moscow or St. Petersburg: in this invitation they would be earnestly joined by the Latins;* the 14,000,000 or 15,000,000 of Eastern Christians, suddenly become Starovirtze, would make common cause with the 8,000,000 Starovirtze of the Russian Empire,† with the 14,000,000 of Latins in Poland and Turkey, and all these would look to the descendant of Osman as their protector.

In prospect, therefore, of a practical occupation of Turkey, some means must be devised for changing

---

* There is a remarkable tendency amongst them at present towards Rome, but it is prompted by the desire to escape from Russian influence through the Church, in the same way as the Christians in Circassia became Mussulmans.

† The number is not known, but in any movement they would unite the Malo-Russians and the Cossacks, estimated at 10,000,000.

the present religious arrangements of the Russian Empire. The Czar cannot reveal himself to the new subjects he expects to acquire under an aspect which, in their eyes, will at once stamp him with the character of Antichrist; and he is placed in the alternative of surrendering a power which himself and his predecessors have laboured during five centuries to obtain, or by some such compact or composition as that to which I refer to break the concert of religious opposition, which otherwise infallibly will be directed against him the moment he assumes the direct administration of the Ottoman Empire. That empire the Ottomans acquired, because they were not Christians; that neutrality which they have maintained in matters of religion and absolute toleration,* they have taught as a habit to their subjects. Russia has promised them something better; they will forget neither lesson. If the power of Turkey fall of itself, its European dominions will present a frightful scene of rage and persecution; but if the head of the official Church of Russia presume to replace it, then will be opened an era from the contemplation of which imagination shrinks; the darkest scenes of the most barbarous ages will be re-enacted; English, French, and German blood

* Passage from "Russia and Turkey."

will flow mingled with that of Russian, Turk, Slaav, and Greek, into the Danube and the Euxine. We shall be called to that field, not as protectors but as gladiators; and Russia, if she does not in the end acquire a second empire, will, at all events, acquire the best thing next to it—she will leave a desert.

Notes of the Editor to the foregoing Essay.

On the 15th of February, 1865, a Report of a Committee was read before the Lower House of Convocation on the subject of communications with a committee of the American clergy relative to "intercommunion with the Russo-Greek Church." It appears from this Report that "an Association has been formed in England, called 'The Eastern Church Association,' which already numbers amongst its patrons the Most Rev. the Archbishop of Belgrade, the Most Rev. the Archbishop of Dublin, with several English Bishops, the principal objects of which are to inform the English public as to the state of the Eastern Churches, and to make known the doctrines of the Anglican Church to the Christians of the East. The Committee has been favoured at their last meeting with the presence of the Very Rev. Archpriests Popoff and Wassilieff, chaplains of the Imperial Embassies of Russia in London and Paris, from both of whom they have received the most cordial assurances of personal co-operation."

Of course they have; this being merely the repetition of the traditional action of the Russian Government, which has repeatedly made overtures of union to the Pope whenever it wanted to make use of him, especially in the time of the Russian struggles with the Order of the Teutonic Knights.

This scheme has originated with Russia, which has taken advantage of the presence of a small party of innovators in the English Church, who have been foiled in their attempt to draw closer to Rome, and who seem to forget that, with the exception of celibacy of the clergy, the Russian Church possesses in a higher degree than the Latin Church what some have chosen to call "the mummeries of superstition." Union, therefore, is impossible. Russia, however, would gain her end by letting herself appear disposed to such an union, by which she would gain some sympathy, and to that extent indifference to her oppression, perhaps extermination, of the Catholics in Poland.

All Russian history is there to show that the Church in Russia has been a political instrument, subject to the objects of State aggrandisement; the religion has become Russian, rather than that Russia has been converted to the religion. Vladimir, the first Christian Prince, would not at once be baptized, but went with an army to Constantinople, as Karamsine says, " to conquer for himself his religion."

At the time of the Crimean war Western Europe was startled by the mention of the God of Russia, and wondered what deity they possessed peculiar to themselves, circumscribed to their country. Karamsine first mentions this divinity in 1380, after the battle of Koulikoff, and mistakenly attributes the words of the conquerors —" The God of the Russians is powerful"— to the defeated Mamaï, khan of the Tatars; a speech which it was impossible for him, who was a Mussulman, to have made, or for his historians to have written.

This phrase gives the measure of their notions of spiritual things, and the way in which they are made to subserve national pride and aggrandisement. The phrase is, however, a remnant of the old paganism as much as a sign of national vanity.

Whilst some in England are imagining that intercommunion with Russia would be intercommunion with the Oriental Church, they would do well to remember that the Moscow Synod is separated from the Patriarch of Constantinople, or head of the Oriental Church, by the usurpations of the Russian Emperors, and that pious and scrupulous Russians, on coming to Constantinople, have to make their peace with the Patriarch, to purge their schism on their own account.

At this moment, too, Prince Couza has commenced a separation of the Church in Wallachia and Moldavia from the Greek Church, by arrogating to himself the nomination of the metropolitans and bishops in those two principalities.

P. 215.—These statements are verified on reference to Karamsine, from whose history it appears that Russia, having been for eight years deprived of a metropolitan by the imprisonment of the Metropolitan Isidore by the great Prince Vasili, on account of the part taken by him at the Council of Florence. Four bishops, as Karamsine says, " in conformity with the desire of the Sovereign, consecrated Jonas as metropolitan, authorised thereto by the blessing of the Patriarch given to that bishop in 1437. But in the circulars sent to all the bishops of Russian Lithuania, Jonas maintains that he had been elected by the bishops of Russia, according to the institutions of the Apostles, and bitterly reproaches the Greeks with respect to their conduct at the Council of Florence. *It is at least dating from this period that we commenced no longer to depend upon the Church of Constantinople, which reflects the highest honour on Vasili.* The spiritual tutelage of the Greeks cost us very dear. During five centuries, that is to say, since St. Vladimir until Vasili the Blind, we only meet with six Russian metropolitans. Without reckoning the presents which were sent to the Emperors and Patriarchs, the foreign metropolitans, always ready to leave our country, heaped up treasures to send them to Greece. They could not bring a very sincere zeal to the interests of Russia, and their respect for our princes could not be as profound as that of our countrymen. These truths were evident; nevertheless, the fear of touching religious matters, by scandalising the people by an innovation in its ancient usages, *had not hitherto allowed the great princes to withdraw themselves from the supreme authority of the clergy of Constantinople.* The disunion of that clergy, on the occasion of the Council of Florence, rendered easy to Vasili the means of doing that which several of his predecessors had abstained from executing from timidity."—KARAMSINE, vol. v. chap. 3, section " *Sage administration de Vasili.*"

P. 254.—It must be remembered that this was written before the commencement of the measures which have led to the crushing of Poland, ending with the persecution of the clergy, and suppression of the Polish convents; which latter measure has been approved of by some in England, as good government.

VI.

ON THE PROTECTION AFFORDED TO BRITISH SUBJECTS AND THEIR INTERESTS ABROAD.

No impartial Englishman, who has travelled much and mingled largely with Foreigners, will deny, that as a nation we are extremely unpopular throughout the world.

One of the most frequent accusations brought against us is, that we are ever ready to bully the weak, whilst we never attempt to do so with the strong; from whom it is asserted, we often put up with slights, and even positive insults, which, as a great nation, we ought to resent.

At first sight there would appear to be some truth in this assertion, when, in looking back, one calls to mind the Sulphur case with Naples, that of Don Pacifico in Greece, and some rather sharp practice with the minor states of the New World.

So much for our high-minded measures, to which is contrasted our extreme moderation in the "Charles et Georges" affair with France; or an equal forbearance shown towards the United States, when Grey Town, then under our immediate protection, was bombarded and utterly destroyed by an American frigate.

We are well aware that there were reasons, and, for the most part, good ones, which induced Her Majesty's Government to exercise severity in the first-named cases and forbearance in the second; but still, as these reasons are not generally known abroad, we are judged of by our acts alone, and hence our unpopularity with foreigners in general.

With regard to our forbearance, that is a matter which solely concerns ourselves; and we can well afford to smile when any doubt is expressed of our ability to resent affronts, whenever we conceive that we have really been insulted.

The charge brought against us of severity towards weaker states is, however, not so easily disposed of: and as that has originated by what is considered as our undue interference in favour of the private interests of British subjects resident abroad, we wish to offer a few observations on a subject so nearly and directly affecting the estimation we are held in by our neighbours; to which we should surely not be entirely indifferent!

As the English are essentially a commercial and trading people, it is natural that British subjects should be found scattered broadcast over the surface of the globe, looking after their interests, and trying to open up new channels for a profitable investment of their trading capital.

As long as they are in the old and highly-civilized nations of Europe they get on perfectly well; and do not, with rare exceptions, give annoyance to their own Government, or that of the country in which they have established themselves, by getting up claims for grievances, more or less founded in fact. When, however, they go to more distant or less settled countries, for the sake of increasing their profits—for such is really the case—then their troubles begin; and then it is that they call for the protection and assistance of Her Majesty's Government against that of the country in which they are either residing, or have founded commercial establishments.

In many cases their claims are founded in justice, but in many more they are brought forward with an outward semblance of right, but in reality as the safe means of getting repaid tenfold the original losses they may have to complain of. It is principally with the weak and dishonest Governments of the New World that the game can be played out successfully, as such Governments generally give rise, by their dishonesty, to some sort of grievances; the reparation for which may then be safely demanded, when backed by the power of such great maritime countries as France and England.

As an illustration of what we mean, we cannot do better than cite a recent instance of such an interference on the part of a strong Government against a weak one in support of a claim such as we have described; and we do so the more readily, as in this instance it was "generous and disinterested France" which was guilty of an act far more arbitrary than any of a similar nature that we have ever been accused of.

Towards the end of the struggle carried on in Mexico, some four years ago, between the Church party and the Liberals, Miramon, as leader of the former, found himself without any funds to carry on the war. Not being able to obtain money from any other quarter, he applied to Mr. Jecker, a Swiss by birth, and established as a banker in the capital of the Republic. This individual consented to "accommodate" the General on the following terms; viz. he furnished him, partly in money and partly in depreciated paper, with 700,000 dollars, for which Miramon, as the head of the Provisional Government, engaged to repay Jecker the enormous sum of 14,000,000 dollars! Shortly after this transaction a battle was fought, in which Miramon was defeated, and the Liberals then upset the Church party and assumed the reins of Government. No sooner was order restored, and Juarez, the chief of the Liberals, acknowledged as President of the Republic by all the principal European nations, than the Swiss banker came forward to claim his fourteen millions! To this demand Juarez naturally enough replied, "No, you have played a game and lost your stake, and you cannot expect us to give you such great profits on money that was lent to our political adversaries to keep us out of power." He did not object[*] to repay the sum actually lent, but refused the fourteen millions. Jecker refused this compromise, saying that he had made a contract with the Government of Mexico, which, whether composed of Liberals or Churchmen, was bound to abide by its terms. He then claimed the intervention of the French Government, and had himself recognised, *subsequent to the transaction*, as a naturalised French subject!

It was this notorious affair that led to the armed interference of France, which has brought about the partial conquest of the country and the placing of an Austrian Archduke, as a sort of French Viceroy, on the throne of Montezuma.

Now we contend that such interference as this ought not to be used in favour even of any *bonâ*

[*] After the landing of French forces in Mexico.

fide subject of a Government so interfering. The matter was one of speculation, and as such should have been left to succeed or fail, according to circumstances as they occurred.

The subject of every powerful nation has an undoubted right to claim the protection of his Government when he is unjustly molested by that of the country in which he may happen to be residing, but we conceive that he cannot call for such interference in order to secure the success of any speculation in which he may engage with such Government.

If Englishmen reside abroad as merchants and traders, it is because they hope to make better profits there than they could do if they remained in their own country; but in voluntarily expatriating themselves for the reason stated, they should be prepared to take the good with the evil.

In most of the minor states of the New World large and profitable speculations can, as a general rule, be made, by entering into contracts with the Government of such states for furnishing arms, ammunition, and accoutrements of all sorts, besides various other things which are required. If these contracts were fairly carried out the profits would, in most instances, be enormous; but some hitch is nearly sure to occur, and then the aggrieved party claims the intervention of his Government in his favour, usually backed at home by some commercial and often political interest following in its wake.*

We would gladly see the system altered, and the rule laid down that henceforward no interference by Her Majesty's Government should be used in favour of any British subject resident abroad, unless he were unjustly molested, either in person or property, according to the laws of the country in which he resides.

* Thus a case is pending in Brazil, a British subject having bought for 7000*l.* a doubtful claim to an inheritance; his right to it has been denied by three Brazilian courts of law, yet he claims an indemnity of 20,000*l.*, and is supported in Parliament by Mr. Newdegate.—*Editor.*

LONDON:
STRANGEWAYS AND WALDEN, PRINTERS,
28 Castle St. Leicester Sq.

www.ingramcontent.com/pod-product-compliance
Lightning Source LLC
Chambersburg PA
CBHW031940230426
43672CB00010B/1992